You, too, can be

FORGIVEN!

You, too, can be
FORGIVEN!

MYRLE MORRIS
with Gwen Young Medina

Whitaker House

Scripture quotations marked (NIV) are from the Holy Bible, *New International Version*, © 1973, 1978, 1984 by the International Bible Society. Used by permission.

Scripture quotations marked (AMP) are from the *Amplified Bible, Old Testament*, © 1962, 1964 by Zondervan Publishing House. Used by permission.

YOU, TOO, CAN BE FORGIVEN

ISBN: 0-88368-082-3
Printed in the United States of America
Copyright © 1978 by Myrle Morris

Whitaker House
580 Pittsburgh Street
Springdale, PA 15144

2 3 4 5 6 7 8 9 10 11 12 13 / 06 05 04 03 02 01 00 99 98 97 96

CONTENTS

Chapter 1

"A Big Mistake"

I was always running away.

When I was a teenager I wanted to do my own thing. Frustrated by parental authority, I ran away from home.

That was only the beginning of my flight. I kept on running. Every time I was crossed, when things didn't flow my way, I would take off. Many times Daddy begged me to quit running away from life's problems and my inability to cope with them. But running away was my only means of escaping life's perplexities.

The time back in the summer of 1968 was no exception. My husband, Calvin, and I weren't getting along. We had a big fight and I ran away, on the spur of the moment, with some old drinking buddies. We went to California and spent three weeks making the round of local bars and nightclubs. We were drunk most of the time. But sometimes I sobered up long enough to hate myself for the kind of life I was living.

I was so homesick and miserable. "Maybe things will be different if I go back home," I thought. I missed Calvin and our son, Calvin, Jr. I even missed his daughter by another marriage, Mary Sue.

"I'm such a failure," I said to myself. "I'm a flop as a wife and a mother. I can't even make it as a human being!"

But when I returned home in September, nothing had changed. I was just as unhappy on the farm in Ohio as I had been in California. Location—a change of scene—was not the answer to my life of sin. Plans of killing Calvin and the children, then myself, began to surface until I could think of little else.

January 1, 1969, would be the day of my death. I wrote the suicide letter in September, shortly upon my return from the west coast. "Let the children have one more Christmas before I kill them," I decided.

A lot of bitter memories crowded my mind that warm September day as I sat, pen in hand and hostility in my heart, writing my final farewell. The house was quiet. Calvin and the kids had gone to town, leaving me alone with my dark and turbulent plans.

"To whomever might be interested," I began writing. "Not that anyone will care," I reflected angrily to myself.

I continued to write, in a hurry to finish before the family returned. Hating myself and the whole wide world, I penned, "Perhaps you are wondering as you look at my dead body and the bodies of my two children and my husband, 'How could anyone do such a thing?'

"Well, it's like this. When you get so low that no one can stand the sight of you because of the way you have lived, and your family hates you and you hate them, and you can't drink enough booze or take enough pills to block out the guilt, then you have to do something.

"I'm going insane, I know. I've known it for

some time. I also know that murder and suicide are sending me to hell. The reason I waited until today to do this is only that I wanted my kids to have one more Christmas. Please don't hate me too much for what I have done. I just cannot go on any longer. We are all better off dead.

"I have had a lot of heartbreak, a lot of regrets. More than anyone will ever know. It's an awful thing to look in the mirror and hate the sight you see. Many of the things that happened to me were my fault. Some were not. Facing reality has been very hard for me.

"I am just no good for myself or anyone else. I've caused enough misery. As you can see, by using Calvin's shotgun, I chose the quickest and most merciful way to end it all. None of us suffered any; it was all over in just a few moments. The children will go to heaven and be better off. Hating Calvin, because he doesn't love me, I decided to kill him, too.

"Everyone will be sorry now for what they have done to me. I wonder though if anyone will even bother to come to my funeral.

"I hope you never forget what you have seen or read here today! I don't want to be like this, but I can't help it. Oh, if only I hadn't taken that first drink! The pain and sorrow I've caused my parents and loved ones, I regret. I can still see the tears in my poor old Daddy's eyes, as he tried to talk to me. But I am past listening to anyone. I'm headed for destruction, and I don't care."

I signed the letter "A Big Mistake."

I folded the white sheet of paper and carefully locked it away in my jewelry box in the top drawer of my dresser. It would be safe there. No one would find it until I took it out New Year's Day.

I went to the kitchen, poured myself a shot of whiskey, gulped it down and cried aloud, "Why was I born?" I smashed the glass against the wall and began to weep.

That was some eight years ago.

Today, I am happy. My past is healed by God's grace.

Knowing His forgiveness and the peace that passes all human understanding has made it possible for me to face the sunrise of each new day, take my responsibilities in hand and get on with the business of living the life He has so lovingly given me.

I think that you will agree, after reading my story, that with God all things are *indeed possible*. And I am talking specifically about the miracle of making something beautiful out of a deformed piece of clay. That was me. Deformed. Myrle Morris: alcoholic, thief, brawler, blasphemer, fornicator, drug user and murderess. With Paul I can readily say:

> "Here is a trustworthy saying that deserves full acceptance: Christ Jesus came into the world to save sinners—of whom I am the worst. But for that very reason I was shown mercy so that in me, the worst of sinners, Christ Jesus might display his unlimited patience as an example for those who would believe on him and receive eternal life" (1 Timothy 1:15-16 *NIV*).

God's gift of forgiveness in Jesus Christ, his Son, has set me free from the inside out. I know I'm an example of His unlimited grace. Believe me when I tell you that I have shared my life with you only for your encouragement and education. God forgives! There is nothing you or I have ever done that will keep us from His incomprehensible mercy. I know. I've been in my own personal hell, but today I'm breathing the air of His pure love.

Today, I stand FORGIVEN! And you can, too.

Chapter 2

Childhood Days

The last time I saw my mother was when I was five years old. She had come to the house of my foster parents when my adoption became final. I still remember her. She had dark hair and large, luminous eyes. She was petite, like my little sister, Jean.

"I brought you and Jean a little surprise," she said softly, handing us each a neatly wrapped gift. Jean and I shyly opened the boxes while our young mother watched us. I noticed how she kept her eyes glued to our every move, as if to store the memory of this moment forever in her mind. How could I know then, or understand why? I only dutifully opened a present from a comparative stranger and murmured my polite thank yous. She'd brought us two little dresses, just alike. I never saw my mother again after that day.

I was born during the Depression on April 29, 1933, in Dayton, Ohio. My father was a French Canadian. He and my mother married when they were teenagers. And my father was too irresponsible to settle down and raise a family. He preferred motorcycles and alcohol to being tied down to a pregnant wife and a baby girl. So they split up.

Although pregnant, Mother hitchhiked, with me on her hip, from Ohio to her people in the hills of Virginia. I don't know whether she was turned away or just didn't want to stay there. But for some reason, she returned to Ohio before my sister, Jean, was born.

When Jean was newborn and I was a year old, she placed us in the Shawn Acres Orphanage in Dayton, and we were sent, soon after, to live in a foster home. The family that opened their hearts and home to us were Charles (Charlie) and Louise Banks. They had one son, Gregg, who was ten years older than I. He would take Jean and me for rides on his pony and draw us pictures. How I adored him!

Sometimes I was very jealous of the attention Gregg gave Jean. He would sit and build block houses, which she would knock down over and over again. I tried a lot of tricks to capture his attention. "Gregg, take me for a pony ride," I'd beg and whine. But his steady blue eyes only gave me a quick glance. "Later, Myrle," he'd say with a grin. He never was aware of my jealous feelings, nor would ever hurt me on purpose.

Jean was the baby of the family. Since she wasn't a healthy child, she got a lot of extra care which I resented. She was dark-complexioned and had dark brown curls. Her big brown eyes enthralled everyone. As for me, I was a large-boned girl with golden hair and green eyes. I loved the out-of-doors; Jean loved to play indoors. She liked to play with dolls and help Mother. I'd rather climb a tree, or race through the meadows around our farm.

My second home with the Banks was a three-story farmhouse known as "Old Bigger Home" (because it

14

was located on Bigger Road). It had many rooms with a fireplace in almost every one, even in the kitchen. The house was divided in half by sliding doors and a big pantry. We lived in the back half and Mother's parents, Grandma and Grandpa Reynolds, lived in the front.

I loved to tag around after Grandpa Reynolds. He would take me to the barn, set me up on one of his big workhorses and let me ride while he plowed the fields. Next to my adoptive father, Grandpa was the most wonderful person in my world. He was big and muscular, with blue eyes that twinkled most of the time. A wad of tobacco was always stuck in his cheek. He never shaved clean, and his whiskers hurt my face whenever he kissed me.

Grandma had cows she milked and fed regularly. I'd always go with her at milking time, because I enjoyed watching the cats trying to get their share of the sweet, warm milk. Sometimes I even helped her with the milking!

One day it was very cold and rainy outside. "Myrle, you stay inside," Grandma said as she opened the back door and headed through the grape arbor for the barn.

"No, no! I'm going with you," I screamed. I was furious and started crying at the top of my lungs. Grandpa, sitting at the kitchen table drinking a steaming cup of black coffee, said, "Myrle, for goodness' sake, hush!" Then, as I continued stomping up and down, he yelled, "Myrle, watch out!" But it was too late. I had forgotten that just behind me were two big tubs of ice-cold water Grandma used to cool her milk cans when she returned from milking. In my temper tantrum, I'd backed into one of them. I was soaked to the skin, and the icy water was such a shock, I quit my carrying on abruptly. It tickled Grandpa's funny bone; I can still see him slapping his leg and the mirth on his face as he laughed raucously until the whole family congregated in the kitchen to view my humiliation.

I was headstrong, even as a toddler, and when the Scriptures say "even a child is known by his acts" (Proverbs 20:11 *AMP*), I have to agree. I never liked being told what to do.

Outside the back door of our farmhouse was a large grape arbor. We had to walk under it to get to the barn. Next to the barn and the water trough stood our big windmill. Across the pasture was a beautiful wooded area. "It's off limits," Mother warned, "until you get to be a bigger girl."

I think I must have been about three years old when I decided I was a "bigger girl." And besides, anything off limits was an invitation for me to investigate, even back then. I was halfway across the pasture on my way towards my objective when I saw a very angry mother pig coming straight for me with her head down. Sows can be very dangerous when they have baby pigs around. I stopped, and fear immobilized me.

Suddenly, my big brother, Gregg, appeared from nowhere—or so it seemed to me—swooped me up into his arms and set me on the pony he was riding. We both watched the mother pig snort and run back in the direction of her little ones. "You little rascal," Gregg said, hugging me close. "You had a very close call." And at the pasture fence, I saw the worried face of my mother who was yelling frantically, "Gregg! Is everything all right?"

"Myrle's all right, Mother," Gregg assured her.

It was too bad, for me, that I never grew close to my foster mother. She was kind to me. She was a slim woman, tall, with dark hair and happy, squinty eyes. Unlike my real mother, who had been in her late teens, my foster mother was more mature. When, as an adolescent, I began my downward plunge, and until my life straightened out some twenty years later, she proved to be a patient, long-suffering woman. Time after time, I caused her and Daddy such acute pain!

Those days of my childhood at "Old Bigger Home" are among my happiest memories. I was attached to that land. I loved as dear, personal friends the tall old pines and the big spreading maple trees that stood majestically around our house. Jean and I spent many happy hours swinging on the tire hung from our favorite maple tree and climbing the old cedar trees together, dreaming of faraway adventures. And it was my delight each spring to gather armfuls of purple violets from the front yard to adorn the tables and dressers in our home.

More special to me than all, however, was my adoptive father. I called him Daddy. He was a short, quiet man, good and gentle. His black hair was straight and combed back from his face. He worked as a factory foreman and at the same time ran a grocery and filling station-restaurant combination called "The Oakdale Grocery." I helped him by washing dishes after school in the back room of the restaurant. But the many long hours and strenuous work loads began to put a strain on Daddy's health. His doctor advised him to slow down. Soon after, Daddy quit his job in the factory and sold the grocery store. "I'm going back to farming," he told my mother.

Daddy worked hard all week, but on Sundays he would sit in the yard, hour after hour, without speaking. He just sat, staring and thinking. "Sometimes, I pray for you, Myrle," he told me. But beyond that, he never shared very deeply with me. I used to long for him to talk to me. If I had only comprehended then what he meant! If I had only known in childhood that there is a God who hears and answers prayer, a God who has a plan for the lives of His children.

Chapter 3

Easy Target for a Dare

When I was eleven years old, my brother Gregg was drafted for service in World War II. It wasn't long before he was shipped overseas. The day he left was very sad, and the whole family went to the train station to wave goodbye. We didn't know if we'd ever see him again.

Soon after Gregg left, I had another sorrow. We had to move from our beautiful country home. "Daddy, why?" I begged for an answer with tears streaming down my face. "Can't we stay?"

"We all hate to move, Myrle," Daddy said. "But the owner is going to sell this house and land. And we can't afford to buy it."

That night I didn't sleep. I lay awake staring into the darkness. Money. We don't have enough money. I learned early in life the power of money.

While Gregg was overseas, we bought a new and smaller home in Beavertown, a suburb of Dayton which is now called Kettering. I never liked our new home very well, and reflecting back now, I think my attitude was unreasonable.

We had an acre of yard and about five acres behind

the house where we built a barn. We also had about five acres of pasture land. Daddy remodeled the house right away, trying to make it comfortable and roomy for all of us. He built an upstairs and remodeled the attic. All the bedrooms were upstairs except one. He also built a large back porch. In the front yard were a number of large pear trees which blossomed so beautifully in the spring.

"It's still not like 'Old Bigger Home,'" I told myself, surveying the finished labors of my hard-working Daddy. And I continued to grieve for the old farm and its familiar woods and pastures.

As far as my religious training went, I wasn't given much choice. We went every Sunday to a Presbyterian church in Dayton. Jean and I used to use our Sunday school money to buy gum and candy which we would eat in the balcony of the sanctuary. While I didn't like going to church, I did learn a lot of Bible stories in Sunday school. It was a fact unappreciated at the time, because I found the whole scene rather boring and couldn't wait to get home. Nonetheless, the information I gained in the house of the Lord was stored in my heart for safekeeping by God's Holy Spirit.

I never related Bible instruction to my daily life. I didn't know I could. I was only aware that I was a gangling pre-teen and not too overjoyed by some of the changes in our lives. Gregg was gone. "Old Bigger Home" belonged to someone else. And my Grandpa had left us. He and another man rented a cabin at Lake St. Mary's where they fished and drank the year around.

I didn't want him to leave; it was a drinking binge that did it. Grandma and Mother were angry with him. He was lying down on the big horsehair-covered sofa in the living room, the smell of whiskey still strong on his breath. He beckoned to me. "Myrle, come and talk to your old Grandpa," he called. I went over and he hugged me. Tears ran unchecked down his cheeks. I guess he had already decided to leave then, but I didn't know it. "Please don't hate me, Honey," he said.

"Grandpa," I assured him with childlike sincerity, "no matter what you did, I could never hate you. I love you."

Soon after, he left. And I was robbed of another companion and friend. So many things began to change. Gregg came home when I was thirteen, and he was so different. His nerves were shot and everything I did and said annoyed him.

Then we got the word that Grandpa was dying up at the lake, and we sent an ambulance to bring him home. From then on, he was bedridden and his doctor gave him a stern ultimatum, "If you drink any more alcohol, you'll die." But we found, every so often, empty whiskey bottles under his pillow. We figured out that the only way he could have gotten them was from the barber who came to the house regularly to cut his hair. In a short time, Grandpa hemorrhaged, and he died one day before the doctor could get to him.

How I missed him! And after his death, my life seemed to go from bad to worse. I was fourteen years old and searching desperately for love. No matter how hard I tried to believe differently, I had always felt that no one really loved me, and that I never really belonged to anyone. It was about this time that my closeness with my sister, Jean, began to end. She was quiet, secure and content at home. I was everything else but! I felt that I couldn't share my inner feelings with her so we just went our separate ways, even though we shared the same bedroom.

I know now my family did love me. They just never realized I was so insecure.

So began my reckless battle for fulfillment. I craved affection, and I was going to get it, one way or another.

Soon after Grandpa's death, I was standing in the hall at school waiting my turn for a music lesson. There were a few other kids milling around, chatting, but I was standing alone, leaning against the wall. Before I realized what had happened, a tall, good-looking boy named Ted walked up to me, took me in his arms and kissed me soundly on the mouth. And then, just as quickly as he appeared, he left without a word of explanation. I was so astonished I almost fainted. My heart was beating so hard I thought everyone must see it pounding through my dress. I later found out that a group of boys had dared Ted to kiss a girl in the school hallway. I just happened to be standing there by myself, an easy target for a dare.

I fell madly in love with Ted, as only a fourteen-year-old can. He was so handsome. Until he kissed me that day, I'd never been kissed before by any boy. I didn't even think about such things. I only thought of boys in connection with trying to outdo them in baseball, climbing trees, riding horses, swimming and rollerskating. But Ted's kiss transformed me. And I worshiped him.

We became inseparable. A good deal of our friendship was taken up with necking, which we did anywhere we could find a secluded spot: in the halls at school between classes, on the bleachers, under the stairways after school. I gave up all interest in study, because all I thought about was Ted. My teachers reported to my parents, who, in turn, were upset and distressed by my behavior.

"Myrle, you're only fourteen years old!" Mother reminded me. "Daddy and I think you're too young to be so serious about a boy."

But I didn't pay any attention; I wouldn't give Ted up. He filled my whole life. Nothing else mattered.

Finally, Mother and Daddy took me out of the school I was attending and paid tuition for me to attend one of the areas "best" schools. Most of the wealthy families sent their children to this school, which had a reputation for providing excellent education and good supervision. I hated it the moment I put my foot in the door. I was from the country, and I didn't feel comfortable with these "city kids." My parents meant well by sending me to school there, but it only increased my desire for Ted.

I became openly rebellious with Mother and Daddy. "Sending me to a different school won't keep me away from Ted!" I shrieked at them one night at the dinner table.

"Myrle, we love you and want what's best for you," Daddy argued. There was such a pained expression on his face.

"We are only trying to help you," Mother said. "We don't want you to be destroyed by being around a boy who is older than you. He's had lots of girlfriends, and he is too fast for you. Some day you'll regret that you had anything to do with him. He can lead you astray and mess up your life."

I just kept repeating angrily, "I love him! I don't care about my education! I don't care about my reputation either. I love Ted, and there's nothing you can do to keep me from seeing him!"

Ted, although he encouraged me in my rebellious attitude, was not as bad as my parents thought. But he was blunt in his estimation of them. "Your parents are old-fashioned and stupid," he would say.

"Yeah," I would agree, "and unfair."

One Friday at school was like a horrible nightmare. And it was, you might say, sort of the last straw. A girl whom I had befriended, and even given a kitten to, found all the combination locks on the girls' lockers opened and turned them backward, and then told everyone, "Myrle did it." About sixteen ferocious girls cornered me in the rest room and began hitting me and pulling my hair. I was rescued by the principal, but the incident made me hate the school even more. That same afternoon, Ted and I made plans to run away together at the first opportunity. A few days later, we met behind the skating rink after school and started out. We took nothing with us.

That first night we took shelter from the early spring rain in an empty house in the process of being built. We sat on the cold, damp floor all night, talking through chattering teeth and shivering from the chill draft that blew in through the cracks.

The next morning, we began walking cross country. It had been raining all week, and we were sometimes in mud up to our knees. We spent the next three days in a hayloft, with no food and only rain water to drink, telling each other of our undying love.

Finally, Ted couldn't stand the hunger and thirst any longer. "Let's give it up, Myrle," he suggested. "It's useless to go on. We'll starve to death."

We were wet and cold most of the time. I was weak

24

but not ready to quit. "Go, if you want," I told Ted, provoked that he would abandon our romantic dreams so soon.

By this time, every man in the county was out looking for us. A posse was formed. We saw them coming and knew instinctively they were searching for us. "Myrle, I'm going. Stay here and see what happens." Ted jumped gingerly from the loft and ran quickly to the other side of the pasture, being careful to keep the hayloft between him and the posse. Then, from the other side of the pasture, from the direction of the woods, he ran toward the men as if coming from behind the trees. They spotted him at once.

The agitated voice of my mother shrilled, "He's killed her and left her body lying somewhere!" (My mother had come with the posse!) When they started giving Ted a rugged time, accusing him of hurting me, I decided to give myself up, too.

Society's justice was so swift! There was a private hearing that same day in the courtroom. My folks demanded that Ted not be turned loose. They knew I'd be right back with him as soon as possible. Ted's parents and the judge decided to make him join the Navy. Ted and I had time for only a few brief words in the courthouse hallway. "Your folks," he told me, "have made such a big stink about our being together this past week that I either have to join the Navy or go to a reform school." His handsome face was lined with helpless fury. "Myrle, I told you what they were like! They're just hicks!"

With youthful stupidity, I agreed. His parents were younger than mine and lived a freer life style. They had to sign for him to join the Navy, because Ted was only sixteen.

As for me, the judge and everyone involved was so concerned for my well being. "Why aren't you happy at home?" the judge asked me. And, "You will have to obey your parents and leave this boy alone."

I just sat there and listened numbly, never saying anything. I was shattered. My heart was completely broken. I believed I would never see Ted again, and I hated Mother and Daddy from the very bottom of my being for causing me to be separated from him.

The judge told me, "We have given you every break. You are a good girl, and we want to help you."

I didn't care what they did with me. But they sent me back home in the custody of my parents. For weeks, I cried many bitter tears, and hate began to fester down inside of me. I became possessed with the idea of humiliating my parents and escaping from them and from Beavertown for good.

Chapter 4

The Runaway

From then on, my parents watched me closely—and with good reason. One night when I wanted to go to the skating rink and they refused to let me, I sneaked out after they were asleep. I rode Daddy's horse to the rink. After having a good time with all the kids, I rode back home, thinking that my parents hadn't missed me.

As I was putting the horse in the barn and was turning around to hang up the saddle I'd just removed, out of the darkness came a horrifying blow across my legs. At first I didn't know what hit me, but I quickly made out the features of my beloved Daddy, a blacksnake whip in his hand. He gave me the first whipping of my life. He didn't yell at me, or talk to me afterwards; he just kept flogging my legs.

Even as a little child, he'd never laid a hand on me. Mother either. They would sit me on a chair in the kitchen and try to talk to me, reason with me. I really believe that was part of my problem; I should have had more discipline growing up. The Bible says you shouldn't withhold the rod (Proverbs 13:24). It was unfortunate for me that they waited until I was almost grown up to start using it. They did the best they knew, but it just didn't work.

The next day at school was embarrassing. I had large, red welts up and down my legs. Some of the kids teased me about it; others sympathized. That afternoon when I came home after school, Daddy met me at the front door, contrition on his face. "Myrle, I'm so sorry," he said. "I wish I hadn't whipped you last night. I realize it didn't help matters much." And he begged me to forgive him.

I wasn't so angry at Daddy. I was sure Mother had needled him into punishing me so severely. But instead of acknowledging that I deserved a good thrashing, I didn't forgive my daddy. I ran away from home. This time, I went alone to the city of Dayton, about fifteen miles from Beavertown. I had a little bit of money left from my school lunches, and I rode the trolley car from the outskirts of Dayton into the heart of the city. I got off the trolley and began wandering aimlessly through the streets. I didn't know where I was going. When darkness fell, I was cold and hungry.

The only person I saw who looked friendly was a parking lot attendant. I ran into him as I was cutting through his lot. He spoke to me first. "Hi!" he called. He waved to me and I walked toward him and smiled.

"Where are you headed?" he asked. He seemed genuinely interested and sympathetic. He said that if I didn't have any place to stay, his wife would be glad to feed me and help me. So I waited around until late that night when he got off work. But instead of taking me home to a loving wife, he drove me out into the country. There, in a secluded area near a dirt road, he raped me. My screams of anguish and terror went unheeded.

When I finally managed to get away from him, I started running. I don't remember much about that flight of sheer terror. I just kept going. When I stopped, I found myself face to face with an elderly man who reminded me of Grandpa. I was crying and talking incoherently.

"Why are you crying?" the old man asked. And when I told him what had happened, he offered to let me spend the night in one of the little cottages making up the motel he owned. He unlocked a cottage for me and brought me some food to eat. About three o'clock the next morning, he woke me up when he crept back into the room and tried to molest me. I fought him off, scratching and kicking, until he locked me in and called the police. He told them, when they arrived, that I had broken into one of his cottages and was trying to stay without paying. The police seemed to know him and apparently believed his tale. I was taken to the detention home in downtown Dayton.

While I was sitting in an outer office, crying and waiting to be interviewed by a caseworker, a police officer sat down beside me and put his arm around my shaking shoulders. From his pocket he took a neatly folded white handkerchief and with it he wiped the tears from my eyes. All the while he clucked soothingly like a mother hen hovering over her babies, "You poor, dear child. I'm so sorry for you. It's all right now. Bless your heart. . . ." He was such a comfort to me, I felt sad when he left.

"What's your name?" I called to him as he walked away.

He turned his kind face for the last time toward me and told me his name. (I don't remember what it was now.) He smiled, waved his hand and was gone. As soon as he left, I was ushered into a little office and cross-examined by a middle-aged caseworker. But I refused to tell her what had happened to me. By that time, I didn't trust anyone. The police called my parents who said they would pick me up the next day. In the meantime, the caseworker questioned me. "Tell me about your life," she said. "And what has caused you to be here?"

I tried to explain. "I loved a boy with all my heart, but my parents wouldn't let us get married. Now I hate them."

"Is that why you ran away from home?" she questioned. As she talked and asked questions, I began to observe her. She was to-the-point and efficient, just doing her job. There was no compassion and no understanding. She was an older woman with an emotionless face. I could perceive clearly that she had already drawn her conclusions. To her, I was a spoiled brat, a troublemaker, and an evil person. Sensing her attitude, I clammed up.

When I left the caseworker, after one lengthy interview, I really wanted to see the policeman again who had taken his time to sit beside me and show me he cared about what had happened to me. I asked for him by name.

"There's no one here by that name," an officer told me.

"Yes," I insisted obstinately, "I've talked to him. I was sitting right over there." And I pointed to the bench where we had sat.

The officer shook his head.

"I know I talked to *someone*," I persisted. I think by then the police officer concluded I was making up a story, so I asked someone else the same question. He, too, said, "Nope. No one here by that name." As the matron was taking me to the girls' dorm, he called after me, "Hey, what does he look like? Maybe you misunderstood his name."

I went back to where he was sitting behind a small desk and gave, what I believed to be, a fairly accurate description. "We don't even have an officer in this station that *begins* to look like that!" He looked into my face and chuckled. "Anything for attention, huh?"

The matron came over and touched me lightly on the shoulder; and I turned and went with her down the hall to the dorm. Suddenly, I had a strange sensation. Who *was* that man? Because of my Sunday school background, I did know that angels sometimes appeared in human form to comfort and encourage. Had I been calmed and cared for by one of God's angels? The idea gave me goose bumps, and I felt a little heartened.

The detention home was just an institution. In my opinion, it's not the place to rehabilitate children. Some of the people I was placed with were hard core criminals. And I was so naive. But it didn't take me long to pick up the lingo.

The one afternoon I spent there, the boys and girls were allowed to play volleyball outside. That's how I met Shep, a young hoodlum with a bullet wound in his leg. He was very proud of that deep scar. He'd already been in the boys' reform school and was on his way home. I guess he took a liking to me, because when we were both near the net, he looked at me and grinned. "Hey, some of us are breaking out of here tonight. Want to go along?"

Did I ever! Anything but going back home.

Later that night, Shep and four other boys overpowered the guard on the boys' floor and then sneaked down to the second floor where the girls stayed. They used the keys they'd taken from the guard on duty and let us out. Four of the girls, including me, went with the five boys.

We stole four cars in our mad flight. We had to, because they kept running out of gas. In the last car, we drove as far as Waynesville, a small town near Dayton. We had an accident there when the car plunged over a steep hill. The car was damaged, but miraculously none of us was hurt! We all climbed out and went up the hill to a barn not far from the accident. Our plan was to hitchhike as soon as the sun came up. It was just before dawn when we opened the barn door and slipped inside. We hadn't been there long when the farmer's wife came down to milk. She heard us talking and ran to get her son, a young man about twenty-one years old. He climbed silently up to the top of the loft and pointed his gun at us. "Get out of the hay," he shouted. "Every one of you, get out!"

We slid quickly off the hay mound where we'd been sitting and talking. "The police are on their way," he informed us. "We'll wait for them." And he kept his gun pointed directly at us.

"You little slut!" the farmer's wife bellowed.

I was quite taken back to see she was referring to me. It seemed I was the one chosen to receive her venom. She kept it up, "You look like you're the one who is the ring leader of this bunch. I hope you get yours! Leading these poor little children astray. Just look at these precious little girls!"

My mouth was hanging open. I couldn't believe what I was hearing. Those "precious little girls" had

32

been in trouble all their lives. They'd been prostitutes, among other things. I was the only innocent person in the group. But this woman was giving it to me right and left. She kept her tireless tirade in full swing until the police arrived. This time, they took us to the county jail.

Awaiting my trial, I saw some ugly sights there. Drunks and prostitutes used foul, vile language. They said obscene things through the door of my cell. It was a vulgar education for a fourteen-year-old girl who, up until the rape by the parking attendant, had lived a fairly sheltered life.

After my trial, a private hearing, I was sent to the Bureau of Juvenile Research in Columbus, Ohio, a place for disturbed children of all ages. I remember when the judge sentenced me. I was so glad I wasn't being sent back home.

The Bureau was a clump of buildings on the same grounds as the insane asylum. The landscaping was attractive and the surrounding area was clean and neat. But inside it was a brutal existence. Again came the barrage of questions, "Why are you unhappy?" "Why don't you want to go home?" I told the psychiatrists there what I told everyone. "My parents don't understand me." It was a typical teenage comeback. And my continuing line of defense was, "I loved a boy and my parents wouldn't let me marry him."

In their study of my habits and behavior, they attached wires to my head to measure brain waves. They wrote daily reports on every detail of my life style. They made notes on how I related to others around me. I slept at night in a large dorm with many beds. And behind our beds was a small isolation room for those who misbehaved. It was also used for newcomers who underwent a series of tests for a week before being admitted to the dorm. I remember that room. I was bored to death. I had nothing to do for a whole week; just lay on the bed. There was no reading material, nothing to wile away the dull hours. Sometimes I peeked out the tiny window in the door, or tried to catch some movement through the small barred window that looked out over a courtyard with a cement slab.

It was indeed a prison for me—that room and that Bureau. I was an outdoor girl: the tree climber, the tomboy. Here we only got outside once a week, even though the state said we should be out a short time every day. But then a lot of things went on that weren't supposed to.

Most of the girls in the dorm were as hard as granite. But I met one girl, Barbara, who was more like me; naive and still unpracticed in the world's vices. God seemed to be watching out for me by giving me a close friend in such a wretched environment. Not that I deserved His interest. But His love is unexplainable. I wish I had accepted it sooner.

It seemed He sent Barbara to me to sustain my sense of balance. She helped me keep my perspective and my hold on reality. We became like blood sisters. No one tired to harm me, or her, because we were always on our guard, one for the other. Every night, before going to bed, we'd kneel down by our beds, bow our heads and say the Lord's prayer.

"Do you mind when the other girls make fun of us when we pray?" Barbara asked quietly one evening as we knelt down.

The thought hadn't entered my mind. With a shrug of my shoulders and a look of utter disdain for the taunts and occasional jeers of the girls in the dorm, I said staunchly, "I couldn't care less! Come on, let's pray."

We didn't really know how to pray in a personal way, but we mustered our best effort by reciting the Lord's prayer from memory. It was another outgrowth of Sunday school teaching.

In spite of the way I treated them, my parents came to see me once a month, on visitor's day. The first time they arrived, they both began to cry. They were so shocked to see their little girl in such a place. I felt sorry for them because they were so heartbroken. "I'm all right," I tried to console them. "It's not so bad here," I lied.

"Myrle, won't you come home?" Daddy lifted his arms in a pleading gesture.

But I still wasn't ready to go back with them. I still held them responsible for all my problems, as unfair as it was. Mother and Daddy returned each month to see me. And they always brought enough candy, cookies and fruit for everyone. The other girls liked to see them coming, because for some, my parents were the only visitors they had. Some children waited all day, sitting silently before the window, staring into space, hoping that someone would come to see them.

My Daddy's tender heart went out especially to one frail, little five-year-old. Sally was emotionally unbalanced. She stuttered and walked strangely. I became her champion, getting into fights with every bigger girl who teased her or asked her questions about what had happened to her and why she was here. I kept her close to my side constantly, protecting her from some who were cruel lesbians. Poor Sally. I found out from the orderlies that her father raped her, and it had shattered her mind. I did what I could. I told her I loved her and gave her some of the things my parents would give me. Even a little red apple meant something exceptional to this forgotten child. And there were others like her . . . innocent little lambs. For them I felt such pity. Sometimes I'd give away everything Mother and Daddy brought me so they'd be happy for a time, anyway.

On Sundays we had church services, but I never got much out of them, although I did attend regularly. I was disgusted most of the time during the sermon, because the older girls sat in the back and deliberately tried to disrupt the meeting. Sometimes they used vile language and told dirty jokes. It angered me. I thought, "How shameful to come to church and curse!" And even though I feared them, I would turn around while they snickered and tell them to hush. Because I wouldn't cower to them, they were always trying to catch me alone so they could beat me up. But Barbara was usually by my side, and I know, too, Someone else was taking care of me. No one ever harmed me. Except once.

Every night, while we slept, a matron sat at the desk outside our bedroom. Through the long and wide window which separated our room from her desk, she could keep an eye on us all night long. One night, I had a nightmare and cried out in my sleep. She walked to my bed and slapped me hard across the face. I was shocked awake and sat up quickly. She shoved me back against the pillow and hissed in a harsh voice, "Shut your mouth! Don't you dare wake up the other girls!" She left and returned to her desk, giving me a malevolent look before she shut the door. I was very shaken by the incident, and didn't sleep too well the rest of the night.

Chapter 5

The Heart Is A Rebel

After three months of testing and counseling, the doctors at the Bureau of Juvenile Research let me make a choice. "You can either go home with your adoptive parents or return to the Shawn Acres Orphanage in Dayton."

Daddy, wanting to persuade me to come home, promised, "Myrle, if you come home, I'll buy you a Palomino colt." He knew how I loved horses; I already had one riding horse of my own. So, to get my colt, I went home with Mother and Daddy. I know now how wonderful they were and how good to me. They disrupted their whole lives for my sake. While I was at the Research Bureau, they moved to another county so I could have a fresh start where no one would know me or know what had happened to me. "We want you to start again," Daddy told me, as we drove to the new house in Warren County.

Our new home was located high on a hill, overlooking the valley below. It was on a lovely farm in the crossroads community of Ridgeville. Mother and Daddy hoped I'd be happy there, and for a while, I was.

It was exhilarating to be out from behind bars, to be free to race my riding horse, Prince, through the fields, to feel the wind in my hair, to breathe fresh air once again. I liked the country town of Ridgeville and made many new friends there. It was a small community with a one-room church, a grocery store and a tavern. That was about it. Living there was wholesome and quaint.

On Sunday mornings, the kids in the neighborhood used to race to get to church first just to ring the bell. I learned how to fish. I went to every ball game. And along with my teenage friends, I skated on the pond, ran laughing through the snow to avoid snow balls and sledded down country roads. In the summer, we went swimming down at the creek where the fresh spring water, as sparkling as clear crystal, bubbled over pebbles and small stones to fill a water hole where we loved to splash and dive.

Mother and Daddy didn't force me to go to church any more. On my own volition, I began attending the little country church in Ridgeville. I went mostly because so many of my high school friends did. Spiritual themes eluded me.

My Daddy kept his word. He bought me a beautiful Palomino colt. I named her Honey Mae, and how I worked caring for her! I washed her down every day and brushed her sleek, golden coat until it shined. I took her for regular walks and made her stretch, holding her head up high with her front legs way out in front and her back feet as far back as they'd go, her ears forward. She was a joy to me, and I was peacock proud when she won blue ribbons at the County Fair in Lebanon, Ohio. In fact, she was the first horse from Warren County, entered from a 4-H Club, to ever win a blue ribbon at the

County Fair! She also won third prize in the halter class as a yearling at the All-American Palomino Show in Eaton, Ohio.

I never did get to ride Honey Mae, although I spent hours getting her accustomed to the bridle and saddle. The day I planned to ride her, I put the stirrups on the saddle. She wasn't used to them. I should have taken her out of the barnyard, away from the other horses, but I didn't think about it at the time. I could see she was nervous over the stirrups hanging quietly by her side as they reflected the sunlight. Her skin rippled. Suddenly, her roan mother—Daddy had bought her for my sister, Jean—came up and nipped Honey Mae on the rump. That did it. She jumped, and when the stirrups hit her on the side, her nostrils flared and she reared up on her hind legs.

Daddy, working nearby, yelled, "Myrle, turn her loose! She'll hoof you!"

I dropped the reins and let her go. She ran all over the barnyard, bucking and snorting. Those stirrups were driving her crazy. She galloped toward the pasture and went through the barbed wire fence, cutting her feet. Daddy and I ran after her in hot pursuit. But we were powerless to help her. I started to cry as I ran while the wind whipped my face, fearing Honey Mae might kill herself. Daddy and I found her laying in a pile of tin cans and broken glass in an area used for a dump. She was torn to pieces. Neither the vet, nor my devotion, could restore her to health. She died of a bone infection several days later.

I was inconsolable. For a long time afterwards, I'd hang on Prince's neck and weep for my beautiful Honey Mae.

At school that year I was popular and well-liked. I'd begun to turn into a very pretty girl. And I had more friends than I'd ever had. It was my love for horses, however, that brought Dick and me together. Jean and I and some of our friends took the Greyhound bus that passed through Ridgeville and went to the race track in Lebanon, about seven or eight miles away. The races were big events in the county. That's where I met Dick, a nice boy with sandy hair and a butch cut. He was in the class ahead of me in high school.

He was racing in a plug horse pony race. (A plug horse is not a thoroughbred.) I saw him sitting tall and straight on his horse as he came out onto the track. Unexpectedly, his horse bucked and threw Dick off. He immediately jumped up, got on his horse again and galloped down the track to win the race.

"Wow!" I thought. "Some guy! I'd sure like to meet *him*!"

That wish became possible when he moved in with his aunt and uncle just down the road from us. We took the same school bus and soon became close friends. We went horseback riding together as often as possible. Soon, we were going steady.

Dick was very popular in school, too, and all the girls liked him. He was a hard working farm boy, and even though he went to school and worked on his uncle's farm, he also had a job after school in an ice cream parlor. He was smart and capable, but his only drawback was he didn't get along with his mother and father. His father drank too much, and that's why Dick went to live with his relatives. Anyway, he preferred the farm to living in town. His mother worked in a tavern in Lebanon and his parents lived above the bar.

I was still a hardheaded teenager usually at cross purposes with my family. And Dick felt sorry for me because I didn't get along well at home either.

One afternoon, I asked Mother and Daddy, "The gang is going to a movie tonight. Can I go?" The town where the movie was showing was about four miles away and they knew we would have to go by car. I guess the idea of a group of teenagers together in a car was something they weren't ready to handle right then, and they said a firm, "No."

That didn't daunt me. I had already made up my mind to go and had an alternate plan arranged. "I'll ask to go horseback riding after supper, just before it gets dark." The rule was I had to have my horse in the barn by nightfall. Mother and Daddy knew I often went out riding after we ate supper, so they offered no objection. In those days, there was no television and people went to bed as soon as the sun went down. Being good farm people, that's what they did. Evidently, they all went right to sleep, even Jean. None of them guessed I didn't plan on going to bed early that night.

Instead, I rode Prince up the road where the kids were waiting for me. I tied the horse to a tree, jumped in the car and took off. "How will you explain yourself if you're caught?" Dick asked, as the other kids quieted to hear my response.

I was pleased with the attention. "Well, when I get home in a couple of hours, I'll just tell them Prince threw me and ran off and I was trying to find him."

One of the girls, Clara Sue, asked, "Do you think they'll believe you?" She looked concerned for me.

I laughed carelessly. "Clara Sue, it will work!"

And it would have, except for one thing. Prince

broke loose from the tree before I got back and went trotting home. He woke everyone up neighing and carrying on. Although it was only about eight o'clock, still early, it was late to my parents. And, of course, it was unusual for Prince to be trotting around the yard since I'd always been careful to see that he was securely in his stall before darkness set in.

Daddy thought the worst. "Maybe she's lying somewhere hurt and injured! We'll have to go search for her." I'd only been gone about an hour.

With visions of the past rolling in like a giant tidal wave, Mother ventured, "Do you think she's run away again?"

Daddy didn't think I'd run away because he knew I was happy at school and busy with friends and activities. He organized a posse and started looking for me. By this time, I'd returned from the movie and found Prince gone. Dick and Clara Sue and the others were afraid to get involved. They let me out down by the creek and took off.

I knew I was in for trouble, and not knowing what to do or where to turn, I hid under the bridge about a half-mile from home. It was pitch black, and I was freezing and scared when I heard, in the distance, the calls of many men shouting my name, "Myrle, Myrle! Where are you?" When they came closer, I knew I would have to give myself up. "They'll find me anyway if I don't," I reasoned. I climbed up the embankment and stood there by the side of the road, waiting for them. A neighbor in the lead spotted me. I was so humiliated and embarrassed. But it didn't help. He was vehement in his judgment. "If you were my daughter," he roared, "I'd beat you to death!"

When I got home I went straight to bed, refusing to answer any questions. Mother and Daddy weren't sure what I'd do if they punished me, and they didn't want to lose me again. So they let it go; it was a pathetic situation.

Dick was sympathetic. "It's too bad you're so restricted at home," he said. We thought we loved each other and soon after this escapade, we resolved to get married. I was sixteen years old and he was seventeen. We borrowed his aunt and uncle's car. They knew we were skipping classes and going to Cincinnati, but didn't know what we were going to do. We got our blood tests and went on to Rising Sun, Indiana, where we were married by a justice of the peace. We were only gone one day, getting back to Ridgeville in the late afternoon. Right away, we went to the ice cream parlor in town where Dick worked and shared with the kids there, "We just got married!" We were so jubilant, so foolish, so childish. Not for one minute did I have a qualm or a regret. I was thrilled that I'd finally gotten out from under the authority of my parents.

Dick and I really never had a chance. We were like two willful children, neither of us prepared for the responsibilities of marriage and children. As time went by, and the first excitement wore thin, we both felt cheated when we saw how much fun our single friends were having. We had mixed feelings about my being pregnant, too. Lynn, our beautiful little girl, was born December 9, 1950, when I was seventeen years old. Dick was so proud of her, and when he came to the hospital, he said, "We have a very lovely little daughter." He smiled congenially, and I knew he was deeply happy.

But it takes more than happy feelings to tolerate the

nitty-gritty of life, and a few months after Lynn was born, we decided to separate. We'd been married about fifteen months. Just before we ended our marriage, I found myself pregnant again—this time, the baby didn't belong to Dick.

Dick and his mother, knowing the baby wasn't Dick's, thought the best thing to do was to get an abortion. Dick's mother made all the arrangements. They drove me to the office of a "quack" doctor who was later imprisoned after a young girl died on his operating table. The room where they took me was dirty, and the doctor was dirty. He repelled me. No one assisted him, and he gave me no anesthetic. I suffered a lot of pain; sometimes it seemed unbearable. Neither Dick nor his mother offered any sympathy when it was over. They helped me in the backseat of the car and drove me home. They believed they were doing the right thing by sticking with me through it.

As soon as I was on my feet again, I divorced Dick and took Lynn to live with Mother and Daddy. They knew nothing about my abortion, and when some months later they found out, they were disconsolate. Even to this day, I sometimes wonder about that child and what he would have looked like, whether it was a boy or a girl.

Soon after my divorce from Dick, I met an older man at the Fair in Lebanon. I was getting off a ride in the amusement park, and he was standing nearby. He began to flirt with me. It was a pickup, and I knew it. But so what? Who cared?

He asked if he could take me home, and I said yes. Harry had a reputation for being fast with women. He'd been married several times. But he was a lot of fun, and we had some good times together, skating, dancing, drinking and making the rounds of Dayton night spots. Our affair didn't last long. He was too bossy. I was too young and wild, and he was trying to settle me down.

"Why don't you wear hose, instead of bobby sox?" Or, "Wear high heels, not saddle oxfords." And when I did get a pair of nylon stockings, he'd nag, "Keep your seams straight!" He wanted me to dress like a woman, instead of a girl. He gave me a diamond, and we were supposed to get married. It wasn't long, however, before we split up.

I went like clock work to the tavern where Dick's mother worked. I wasn't old enough to legally drink, but the bartender there knew me because of Dick's mother, and he gave me drinks to keep me around. It was good for business to have a pretty, young blond sipping drinks at the bar. Another favorite hangout of mine was another bar in Lebanon. I didn't have trouble buying drinks there, either.

In those bars, I met a number of girls who used to go to school with me. I wouldn't have anything to do with them in high school because they lived in a bad section of town and had scandalous reputations. But since none of my old friends would have anything to do with me— their parents wouldn't allow them to even talk to me—I started running around with these other girls, some of whom were prostitutes and shoplifters. I didn't blame my former schoolmates. At seventeen, I was a divorcee, a murderess, a kept woman and a thief. Thank God, Lynn had a home with Mother and Daddy. They adored her. In those early years, she grew up not knowing me as her mother, but rather as an older sister who stopped by now and then to inquire for her welfare.

I stole a lot of baby clothes for Lynn after I learned how easy it was to shoplift. And I also swiped jewelry from a big Dayton department store and sexy cocktail dresses for my drinking sprees.

Between getting money from men and stealing, I dressed well. I had matured and ripened into an attractive and well-formed young woman. But when I looked into the mirror, I didn't like what I saw. I knew that hidden behind that pretty face and those golden curls and vivacious green eyes was something evil that I seemed to have no control over. Wild parties and unruly men were all I lived for. And I had very little time for my darling baby girl or anything else worthwhile.

Chapter 6

Shifting Sand

In a bar in Franklin, Ohio, I met a man who could outdance everyone I'd ever known. Jim had just been discharged from the paratroops and there was an instantaneous chemistry between us. By the time he said, "Myrle, let's get married," I'd been divorced only a few months. I thought it was time to find a new husband, so I said, "Yes!"

Daddy gave us a half-acre of land on his farm. For Jim and me, it was like a little piece of heaven. We built a cute little cottage and settled down to married life. A year later we had a black-haired, blue-eyed baby boy whom we named Tommy. Two years later, Kevin was born, then two years after that we welcomed Gregg (named after my brother) into the family. Lynn, my little daughter, was also a part of our happy household from time to time.

And we *were* happy. At least for a while. Jim had a good job in a factory in Dayton. And our future was secure—or so we thought. Jim was a wonderful father. No matter how tired he was when he came home from work, he always found time to laugh and play with the kids. Once he came through the front door so exhausted; he'd been working two eight-hour jobs. Tommy ran to him, bouncing and skipping, full of toddler vitality. "Daddy, Daddy!" he said. "Please, won't you saddle the pony so I can go for a ride?"

Jim couldn't resist the blue eyes of his firstborn, and even though he was so weary he could hardly move, he took a deep breath and said, "Okay, Son." He smiled. "Let's go for a ride."

He not only saddled the pony, but led it around and around the field, with Tommy squealing in delight and relishing every moment.

Jim liked to take me out for good times, too. He loved taking me "barhopping" and once a month we went dancing. Life was pretty smooth until shortly after Gregg was born. Then came the lightning bolt! Jim was laid off work, and no other jobs were available anywhere. We drew $40 a week in unemployment pay, but that didn't go far, not with three babies to feed and clothe.

We had debts, too. We couldn't make our payments on the furniture and car, to say nothing of our house. One night after the children had been bathed and put in bed, Jim put his head in his hands and declared, "Myrle, we're going to lose everything."

There was nothing I could think of to say. I was uneasy and apprehensive. "What will happen to us? What will we do?" was all that came to mind. Unfortunately, Jim and I began taking our financial crisis out on each other. We grew further and further apart. Adding coal to the fire, I started flirting with a married man in town. Jim was insanely jealous; he began accusing me of things I hadn't really done. I was so vexed by his accusations that I did a hideous thing. I invited this man up to our house one night when Jim was away. Somehow Jim discovered my affair, and he started chasing other women to get even.

One night I followed him in the car to a house of prostitutes. My heart was pounding like a trip hammer; rage made my face hot and flushed. Parking the car about halfway down the block, I walked with determined steps toward the house where he'd gone. An outside stairway led up past a window. I climbed the stairs, looked through the pane and gasped at what I saw. There, inside a brightly lit kitchen, was my husband and another woman, embracing! I exploded in fury and kicked the window in, cutting my leg to the bone. Then I shrieked, cried and flailed my arms like a mad woman. Everyone in the house came racing out onto the lawn to see what was going on. Jim appeared and stared at me incredulously.

Before I knew it, the girl who had been with him came at me like a tiger, scratching, kicking and yelling obscenities. No one moved to help me until the old woman who owned the house cried out, "Get that young woman to the hospital! She's bleeding to death, and I don't want a corpse in my front yard!" There was blood from my wound everywhere.

I was in bad shape, and Jim and another man rushed me to the emergency hospital. I looked at Jim's face on the way to the hospital, and it was a mask—no emotion and no remorse. We didn't say a word to each other. While I was in the hospital, Jim took the children to my mother's house, packed a few belongings and went to live with the woman I'd seen him with. When I got home three days later, I drove to where he was. I honked the horn, and he came out the door. He walked over to the car.

"Get in," I said quietly. "We need to talk."

"What about?"

"Never mind. Get in and talk to me."

We talked for a time, and I begged, "Jim, come home with me. Let's forget the past. Let's put it behind us. What's done is done. Let's go on from here. We have three good reasons to try and make it: our boys, your children."

His face softened. He went inside, gathered his clothes and came home with me. But I couldn't forgive him. All I could remember was seeing him with someone else. It was a portrait painted indelibly in my mind. I couldn't forget. Although I made all kinds of excuses for myself and the affair I'd had with another man, my heart was not generous enough to pardon Jim for the same mistake. I decided to call it quits, and Jim and I separated two weeks later on Tommy's fifth birthday.

Jim left, and I was alone in our memory-filled cottage. It was more than I could bear. I tried to stay there and be a good mother to the children, but I couldn't stand the quiet and solitude. Every evening, I found myself waiting for my husband to come home from work, remembering how he always found time to play with the children, no matter how tired he was. I gave up after a few days and moved in with Mother and Daddy. Of course, I should have known better. It didn't work.

"I have got to find another life for myself," I told Daddy one summer day about two weeks after Jim and I parted. "The kids will be better off with you and

Mother. You love them, and Mother wants to take care of them. I think the best thing for me to do is move to Dayton and get a job."

"Myrle, we'll do all we can to help you," Daddy said. "You know that." His gentle eyes were moist and he fumbled around in his pocket for a handkerchief to blow his nose.

I sold my house in a matter of days and left the children with my long-suffering parents in Ridgeville. I only hoped the excitement of a big city would crowd out the past and give me some reason to go on living. I was twenty-three years old.

Chapter 7

The Tall Stranger

Six years is a long time to live with a man, then abruptly be deprived of his companionship. To fill my emptiness, I headed for the bars in Dayton where I used to go dancing with Jim. The girls who worked in these bars, mostly prostitutes, didn't welcome me with open arms as they had when I came with my husband. Now I was competition, and they hated me. When I'd get up to dance, they'd try to knock me off the floor. One night a bleached blond strutted by where I was drinking at the bar and sputtered in my ear, "If you get up to dance again, I'll kill you!" In her hand was an open knife. She saw my terror and gave me an evil smirk.

I went immediately to the bouncer and told him what had just happened. He laughed contemptuously. "You're a big girl now," he said. "Take care of yourself!"

As I left the bar late that night, several girls who "worked" the streets, rolling drunks or soliciting customers, jumped me. They would have beaten me to a bloody pulp if a man passing by hadn't rescued me. It was another incident I pondered years later. The man appeared as if from nowhere, commanded the girls with a strong, authoritative voice to leave me alone, got me to my feet and called a cab. He helped me into the taxi, put some money into my hand and was gone before I could thank him. I'll never fathom the goodness of God; it's absolutely unmerited.

After that, I was involved in at least one fight a day for a period of a year or more. I had a chip on my shoulder, and whenever one of these girls said anything derogatory to me, I'd slug her! The police arrested me so often for drunk and disorderly conduct they began to tease me about becoming a lady wrestler.

When I moved to Dayton, I shared a shabby apartment in a depressed area with Anna, a prostitute and a drunk. When she was sober, she was kindhearted to those she knew. But when she drank, nothing mattered to her. Not even her two little boys. One was five years old, and the younger was four. Sometimes she forgot to feed them; so I did. People in the neighborhood complained because the kids were running the busy downtown streets and anyone who came along was trying to give them food.

Anna had a sad past. "I used to go to church with my Mama as a little girl," she told me once between drinks. "I was a pretty little girl," she added with a melancholy smile. "But I married the wrong man and got away from Jesus. We left our home in the mountains of Virginia and came to Dayton, had two children...." Her voice trailed off.

I was lost in my own memories of church and kids and married life. So far, I'd made a dent in this world by doing all the things the church frowned upon. "Anna, you never told me what happened to your husband," I said.

"He left me," she stated casually. "It's funny," she went on, "he got me to drinking, and then I couldn't stop."

I knew underneath she really cared; she had loved him. I felt deep sorrow for this woman and myself. But what was the answer? I think I bawled as much as Anna that year when they came and took her boys and put them in an orphanage. It only added to her problem, because then she quit caring whether she lived or died.

The agony of loose living continued and the days blended into one another until I lost all track of time. Periodically, an incident here and there would stand out as a bright light against the blur. Like that one night when I was sitting in a very dirty bar, drinking. A man walked in who looked familiar, a face out of the past. But where? Where had I seen him before? Trying to focus my eyes, I staggered from the booth where I had been sitting to the bar where he was ordering a drink. To my utter surprise, he stood up as soon as he saw me, grabbed for my hands and pulled me towards him. "Myrle," he exclaimed, "I've been looking for you!"

I recognized him and began to cry. "It's you! Ted!" It was my first boyfriend, after ten long years. "How did you know where to find me?" I managed to say, wiping my tears.

"I met a guy who used to go to school with us. He's a cabdriver, and he told me where you were."

I laughed. "I guess I do come in this bar a lot." But I still didn't understand. "Why did you come? Why were you looking for me?" I was so ashamed that he had found me in such a place, and looking the way I did.

"I want to talk to you," he explained. "Come on. Get your coat. Let's go for a walk."

We walked a long, long time through the streets, up one block and down the other. He told me he was married but had heard how I was living. "I just had to come and see if there was any way I could help you," he said. Although he told me he would always be my friend, we both realized that too much water had gone under the bridge for us to try and make it together. A few hours later we parted—this time forever.

Seeing Ted again brought back a flood of bitter memories. It resurrected the past, and I despised myself for the direction my life was taking. I drowned out reality with more liquor.

While I was on the "street," I ran with a motorcycle gang and dated the leader. He was rough and handsome. All the girls wanted him. His self-centered life, however, didn't turn me on, and I decided to look for another boyfriend. That's when I met Slim. One night in a tavern, a tall stranger walked towards me and asked me to dance. I accepted. He talked with a low southern drawl and was very tan. He said he worked on construction in the area. The magnetism between the two of us was powerful, like electrical shocks. And when he asked me for a date, I said, "Okay!"

The night of our date rolled around, and I was drinking and having a blast at a local bar, or so I thought. I had forgotten all about Slim until he walked in, took me by the arm and led me out of the bar. "Look," he said. "I feel so sorry for you, Myrle. I know you can't be happy living the way you do."

I started to cry and began telling him all my troubles. He was kind. "Would you like to go to the country and see your children?"

I nodded. He bought me some black coffee, which I hated, and sobered me up a little bit before driving me home to Ridgeville. My little ones were thrilled to see me. They hung on my skirts when I started to leave. "Can't you stay with us, Mama?" Tommy asked, pitifully.

I tried to smile, but it dissolved on my face. I knew it was useless to try and explain to this child why I couldn't stay. It was impossible. There were too many memories. It would drive me up the wall. Even standing there, saying goodby to all of them, reminded me of the times Jim and I had gone to the little one-room church with the kids, of the picnics we used to have together, and of the many nights when the children were sick and we were both up with them all night. How proud he'd been when the babies were born, and he had hovered over each one. "They all look like me," he'd say. It was odd; I could remember only the happy moments. Now they were gone forever—and I didn't know what in the world was going to become of me.

It had been raining that night. The atmosphere was dreary. I was so lonely, and Slim was so kind that I decided to let this stranger be the center of my attention for a while.

Chapter 8

Beyond My Reach

For almost two years, Slim and I went together and lived together off and on. It was a tumultuous, stormy affair. While I tried to hold down a steady job working in a factory on a mill machine that cut little steel parts, he tried his best to keep me out of bars at night by taking me to movies three or four times a week.

My job was only bearable because of a compassionate foreman. He counseled me often and tried to give me advice. "Myrle, you have such potential," he'd say. "So much possibility. You're such a good worker, too." He wanted to see me happy, he said, because he knew I was very unhappy and had a drinking problem.

"Slim keeps you in such a constant state of torment, you ought to give him up," he told me over and over again. He saw me come to work so many mornings in tears, and I'd always end up crying on his shoulder. Finally, one day, he said, "Take a sick leave and go visit your kids. Try to get yourself together."

I did take the sick leave, but I never made it to Ridgeville. For six weeks, when I should have been loving my little babies, I was in a drunken stupor. Just before I went back to work, Slim took me to see the movie "King of Kings." I was so impressed when Jesus was captured and mistreated. He never fought back, but let His tormentors have their way with Him. Why? It broke my heart when they killed Him, nailing Him to the cross! Why did He die? I didn't really get the spiritual implications. If only I had!

That night I went home alone, because I needed to have time to think. The movie had started me pondering serious questions. I did want to change my life, but didn't know how. I tried to pray. "God, I'm so sorry for the way I am. I don't want to be like this." And I sobbed late into the night, eventually falling asleep close to daybreak. When I woke up, I didn't feel any different. I headed for the bar and with guilt feelings ordered a drink before going to my job at the factory.

It was strange, thinking back on it now, that Slim confessed to me that his folks were Christians. "They love the Lord," he told me, "and they are having a fit about our adulterous relationship." I was sorry about it, sorry that they knew, but didn't care really. Slim and I were at odds so often, arguing and fussing over one thing or another.

One night on the way home from a movie, we had a big blowup over something. Slim angrily slammed on the brakes and let me out of the car in the alley back of the bar where we went for drinks at least three or four times a week. Everyone parked their car out back in the alley, and it was well lit. We had used this back entrance many times.

Slim screeched away leaving me to go in alone. I had my hand on the doorknob when I was startled by someone grabbing me forcefully around the neck. I couldn't even scream. I felt a sharp pain in my back and a low, excited voice close to my right ear rasped, "Don't turn around, or I'll stick this knife clean through ya."

Panic, fear and helplessness smothered me as my assailant threw me down a flight of steps leading to the basement of the tavern. He raped me, abusing me terribly. Just as he raised his knife to kill me, and while all time seemed suspended, he changed his mind and raced up the stairs. I started climbing the stairs on my hands and knees and got a good look at him as he passed under the bright light of the bar's rear door. He was a young, black man and I knew I would never forget his face. Crawling up the cold cement stairs from the dirty floor at the bottom, I struggled to get the back door open before I collapsed. I was crying hysterically. A detective was leaning against the counter, and he took one look at me, then ran with gun drawn into the alley. He found no one.

It was six weeks before I was emotionally able to go back to work. I felt so dirty inside, my nervous system was nearly destroyed. While I recuperated, the police had me look through thousands of mug shots, but the black man's picture was not among them. Three months later, the same detective walked into the bar where I was with a picture of a fellow who had been paroled from the penitentiary in New York. One look at the photo and I knew it was the same man who had attacked me.

"Thank God, we've got him now," the detective said, explaining, "The guy has accosted over thirty women. He killed one, and that's how we got a lead." He looked at me for a moment, quietly.

"What's the matter?" I asked.

"We know where he's holed up, Myrle. You're a key witness that he's our man. Will you go with me while I make the arrest?"

I didn't hesitate. "Yes. Let's get the creep behind bars."

He was eventually tried, convicted and sentenced to a life term.

As far as Slim and I were concerned, we were still lovers, but our relationship was becoming more and more strained. The only reason Slim reconciled with me, time after time, was so he could sleep with me. Later, he would run out on me again. To him, I was only a body. Tragically, I needed him for deeper reasons than just fleshly lust. I think my demands for loyalty scared him. But his conscience got the best of him one day, and he asked me to marry him. At first, I was so happy. I was sure he loved me as much as I thought I loved him. We set the date for our wedding, and I took the day off from my job at the factory to meet him at the courthouse. We planned to get our license and find a justice of the peace to marry us. We met on the courthouse steps.

"Well, we're going to get married," Slim said, in a pensive mood.

"Yes," I answered happily, feeling giddy like a delighted child waiting for Christmas morning. I looked up into his face and saw, for the first time, the trouble brewing in his dark eyes. My bubble of happiness burst.

"I'm not going to promise you it's going to work," he said. "In fact, I don't think it will."

I couldn't do anything but stare at him, not believing this was happening to me on the day of my wedding! He continued, "Myrle, I don't want any children and you have four. I don't think I'll make a good father. I think I'll always be jealous of your time with your kids. My family will never accept you, either. But," he shrugged his broad shoulders with resignation, "I'll go ahead and marry you anyway. I think I owe you that."

I finally found my tongue and yelled at him. "You don't owe me nuthin'!" and I began to cry. I flipped around, flew down the steps and ran back to the two-room apartment we had shared. To my disgust, Slim showed up within minutes and tried to make love to me. Wishing desperately that I was the decent girl his parents wanted him to have, yet feeling used and rejected, I grabbed a kitchen knife and stabbed him. I meant to kill him, but only sliced his arm as he raised it to protect himself.

Then, blinded by violent rage and tears, I ran out the apartment door and into the street. A drizzling rain, matching my low spirits, drenched me as I walked and stumbled along the sidewalk. To get out of the rain, I took shelter in a Catholic church where candle light flickered against the walls and ceiling. It was so spacious and beautiful inside! I'd never set foot in a Catholic church before and for a moment, I was overcome with its beauty and cathedral-like splendor. I dropped to my knees on a kneeling bench, and not knowing how to pray, I simply sobbed, "Please, dear God, help me!" I was sure God was there somewhere, but I didn't sense any answer to my immediate need. I got up and left, as impetuously as I had come.

I felt I could never live with Slim again, and yet I had become so dependent on his companionship that life without him seemed emptier than ever. I walked with these heavy thoughts into the roughest bar in Dayton at that time: the Spur Bar. Pushing my friends away from me, I threw a sugar shaker to the floor, picked up the sharp bits of glass and slashed my wrists.

"Oh, God, if I could only die," I moaned. But I didn't die. The bartender called the police; it was an unsuccessful suicide attempt.

The next day I quit my job in the factory and with the memory of my boss's kind face and his parting, "Myrle, there'll always be a job here for you," I drove to Middletown, Ohio, to try and forget the tall stranger who left me still seeking for a love that always seemed just beyond my reach.

Chapter 9

The 900 Club

One of the best things that ever happened to me in Middletown was Calvin. I can say that now because Calvin is not the man he was when I first met him. Nor am I the same woman, for that matter. He, like me, was a sinner saved by grace. But when I first met him, almost twenty years ago, he was a bartender in a little Middletown tavern. It was Sunday when I drove into town in my secondhand Plymouth. So I was looking for a bootleg bar. In Ohio the bars couldn't sell whiskey on Sunday. At a bootleg bar they'd draw their shades after hours and on Sundays, and people like me would sneak in and drink hard whiskey until the bar opened the next morning.

That's how I met Calvin. He and his cousin ran a tavern—the 900 Club. Calvin was the bartender. That Sunday I got very drunk, and Calvin let me sleep it off upstairs in his room. The next morning he brought me breakfast. It was the first time anyone had ever thought of feeding me. After that, I was like a little puppy tagging along beside him. I needed the human goodness of this man.

From then on, I made the 900 Club my headquarters. It was a rough place and always full of rowdy people. Fights were frequent, and I soon learned that just about every ex-con in the area hung out there. But I liked the excitement because it helped me forget Slim and the fact that I had four little ones being cared for by a mother and father I couldn't seem to forgive.

I was glad to be away from some of those bars in Dayton, too. I was exceedingly thankful to be away from the little old lady who used to stand outside the bars for hours, no matter what the weather, waiting for me to come out. She was short and frail with a tired way of standing, as if she was so weary. But on her face was a heavenly glow, a light from another world. It always brightened when she saw me.

Time after time—patiently, lovingly—she would take hold of my arm, look deeply into my eyes and, it seemed to me, deeply into my scarred and wounded past, and say, "Jesus loves you. Would you let me help you?" I got sick of hearing about Jesus' love. I did appreciate the caring that made this frail old woman stand on the street day after day, but I tried studiously to avoid encountering her because I didn't know what to say to her when she went through her routine about God. I had too much respect for the name of Christ to spurn her openly.

Many times she'd say to me, "Why don't you come home with me? Let me take care of you so you don't have to live like this." She was so sweet and kind, I'd have to break away from her and run down the street so she wouldn't see me crying and know how profoundly she'd touched me. Well, at least in Middletown I didn't have to worry about running into her anymore.

68

I liked Calvin, the bartender, from the beginning. He would buy me drinks and make all the other men in the bar leave me alone. He felt sorry for me. "Myrle, you never sleep," he said to me one day as he shined a glass behind the counter and placed it on the shelf above the bar.

"Sleep?" I chuckled.

"You look sick," he continued. "Do you feel all right?"

"Sure," I answered lightly. "I feel fine." It was not a convincing reply, not even to me. I seldom slept, except in a booth or on a bar stool, with my head down on my arms. I rarely ate, except when someone offered me a sandwich—and that never seemed often enough.

I'd been hanging around the 900 Club for a couple of weeks when Calvin asked me to take him into the mountains of Kentucky to get the rest of his clothes, since he didn't have a car. "I didn't bring them all with me when I left," he explained. As we drove to Morris Fork, he started telling me tales of his childhood days, his grandparents, his dog, Spot. At one point, tears spilled down his face as he reminisced. I saw then that this man had been as deeply hurt as I had been, and that he wasn't as tough as everyone thought—at least not on the inside. I saw that Calvin had been through as much in his lifetime as I had in mine. It made me feel close to him.

When we returned from Kentucky, Calvin gave me a place to live over the 900 Club—his tiny, filthy room over the bar, just big enough for a dresser and bed with a burned mattress. There were no sheets to cover the burns. I have no idea how many nights I lay passed out on that mattress, my head hanging over the side of the bed.

One morning, as I looked up at the ceiling, I saw things that weren't really there—wiggly creatures, like a bunch of spiders—and they began dropping down on me. Usually I was so sick it was difficult to stand up, but as soon as the doors opened downstairs, I'd be on a bar stool, trying to keep down that first drink to get rid of the "shakes." Some nights I'd take an extra bottle upstairs with me, to help me get on my feet the next morning.

After a few days, that dirty little room became a love nest for Calvin and me. Even though he drank and was sometimes very cruel, I found that Calvin had a big, generous heart. He was one of the few men I'd met in a tavern who seemed interested in me as a person, not just as a body. We became very loyal friends, as well as partners in sex, crime, drinking, and fighting.

Calvin was, like me, an alcoholic. But he was intolerant of my drunkenness. When he got drunk, he would beat me for getting drunk. I'm not sure I loved Calvin at that time. But I do know that I needed him and he needed me. I found myself becoming more and more dependent on him. He fed me what meals I ate, bought my clothes, and shared my bed. When we had been living together only a few months, I became pregnant. About the same time, an incident occurred that was to close the doors of the 900 Club.

There was a fight, which in itself was not unusual. But this was different. Some men got in an argument at another bar in town and chased one of the fellows to the 900 Club. The young man on the run knew Calvin, and came to him for help. "They're after me, Calvin," he said with a trembling voice.

70

"I don't want any trouble," Calvin told him. "You'd better get out before they find you here."

"You don't understand! They're going to kill me!" He no sooner finished telling Calvin that he feared for his life when six or seven men walked in the back door. "We're going to kill you!" one man shouted. And another one said, "I'll go to the car for the gun."

The young man looked at Calvin with imploring, terror-struck eyes. "Help me!" he cried.

I could see and hear everything, because I was sitting at a table in the middle of the room. Everyone in the bar had quieted down, wondering what would happen next. Calvin yelled at the men near the back door, "If you bring that gun in here, we'll kill *you!*"

The men lunged for Calvin, so he grabbed a heavy club he kept under the counter and started hitting them over the head, trying to edge them all the time toward the back door and out the tavern. While he was working them over with his club, Calvin's cousin came in the front door, saw that Calvin was in trouble, and shouted, "Stop, or I'll shoot!" and he pulled a revolver from his coat. The guys kept on slugging Calvin, and he kept on pounding them. So his cousin fired a shot and the bullet went through one of the men from back to front, glanced off the wall and landed right on the table where I was sitting! It didn't even slow the guy down; he kept right on punching. But his friends got him out the door and into the car and took him to the hospital.

Fortunately, he lived. But the judge closed the bar for a short time because, he said, "You have too many fights there and too much trouble." And, of course, he was right.

71

Chapter 10

The Mountain Man

God's grace is indeed something to contemplate. Because even in Calvin's childhood, as in mine, there was always that spiritual training that continued to haunt him when he grew up and left home. Calvin was born in 1928, about thirty miles from Jackson in the heart of the Cumberland mountains. He entered this world in a tiny, two-room cabin in a mountain hollow called Morris Fork one cold Christmas Eve.

When his mother died a few years later of tuberculosis, his father took him up the hollow to live with his parents, Jeff and Mary Morris. Calvin's granny was a Christian who loved Jesus with all her heart. She taught him scripture verses and told him Bible stories in front of the fireplace. When he was eight years old, Calvin made a commitment to the Lord. He attended church and Sunday school every Sunday, even winning awards for perfect attendance. The preacher in the Morris Fork church then was Sam Vandermeer—"Uncle Sammie," as he was lovingly called by everyone in Morris Fork— and his ministry played a leading role in Calvin's childhood growth and development.

Grandpa's modest four-room mountain home was made of logs, which were later covered with siding. The kitchen and a back bedroom were heated by the cooking stove; the other two rooms were heated by fireplaces. Water was drawn in a bucket from a well outside the back door. Many times in the winter, Calvin would have to break the ice off the bucket of water in the kitchen before drinking it or washing in it. Across the front of the house is a porch where Calvin and his grandparents spent many hours talking and working— Granny quilting, snapping beans, or rocking in her old chair; Grandpa swatting flies; and little Calvin whittling with his knife.

Calvin's youth was lived in the out-of-doors. He was a real woodsman with a kind, gentle spirit. He was a hard worker. During the growing season, the whole family—Grandpa, Granny and little Calvin—would hit the hills every morning at sunrise with hoes in hand. Granny would get up around four o'clock and cook breakfast on a wood-burning stove. She could outwork most men in the fields and would always take the "lower row," which was the hardest to hoe on the side of the mountain. Little Calvin sometimes complained of being tired, and she'd say, "Well, Honey, we'll quit and rest awhile when we get to the end of this row." Her back bent, with hoe in calloused hands, around and around the hills they'd go until suppertime.

Calvin's grandmother loved as hard as she worked. Even today, if you mention the name of Mary Morris to the older people on Morris Fork, there will be a smile and a moment of hesitation as their minds wander back. Then they nod and say, "Yes, old Mary was a wonderful good woman," each one remembering times his family

74

had been sick or in trouble and Mary had sat up all night with them. To get to their homes, she sometimes had to walk many miles through mountains that men today wouldn't try to cross without a pack and supplies. Slinging over her shoulder a potato sack loaded down with things she'd prepared, off she'd go with little Calvin and his squirrel dog, Spot.

Grandpa used to make "moonshine" back in the 'thirties, and people from everywhere would come on mule and horseback to buy Jeff's good liquor. Granny, being a Christian, didn't approve of "moonshining," but knew she couldn't go over her husband's head. When anyone came to buy whiskey, however, she would take his gun and keep it until he was ready to leave.

One night Grandpa suddenly woke up out of a sound sleep. Coming out on the front porch, he looked across the front yard and saw a figure in white standing on the creek bank. "It's the Lord Jesus!" he exclaimed. He was so shocked, he ran back into the house and woke up Granny. "I just saw the Lord!" he shouted into her sleepy face.

"What are you going to do about it?" was her simple, matter-of-fact response.

"I'm going to get right with the Lord," he answered. "I'm not going to sell whiskey any more either!"

"Praise the Lord!" said Granny before she went back to sleep.

Grandpa meant what he'd said. In the next few months, he destroyed his stills where people used to ride for miles around on mules and horses just to buy his booze. He quit drinking and began to live for the Lord. It was Granny's greatest joy when, after so many years of walking with the Lord, she now could share spiritual things with her husband.

As a boy, Calvin loved to hunt squirrel and rabbits and spent many hours—sometimes days—in the woods alone with his dog and his God. In the fall, he'd take off across the mountains with his gun and Spot. Together they crossed creeks and ravines, the boy swinging across on wild grapevines and the dog getting across the best way he could.

Because very few high schools were built in the Kentucky mountains, a student who wanted to further his education beyond the eighth grade had to pay to go to school in another part of the state. Many families—including Calvin's grandparents—couldn't afford this expense. But it didn't deter Calvin's love for knowledge. He studied his lessons by firelight or by the light of a kerosene lamp. He loved reading and borrowed many books from the school library.

At the age of fourteen, when he finished the eighth grade, Calvin said goodbye to Grandpa and Granny and walked to Indian Creek—about six miles away—then hired a man to take him to Beattyville, Kentucky. From there he took a train to Lexington and then a bus to Covington. Across the creek from Covington is Newport, Kentucky, where Calvin's Aunt Minnie lived. It was there that Calvin decided to settle and go to work.

Life in Newport was much different from life in the mountains. Newport was a wide-open town in the 'forties, and Calvin was right in the middle of the excitement. Turning his back on all his Christian upbringing, he tended bar, ran a few card games, and adopted most of the vices he was exposed to—notably gambling and drinking. In Newport, Calvin met and married his first wife. He later joined the army and was shipped to Japan. His oldest son, Douglas, was born while Calvin was overseas. Before he returned to the States, his wife divorced him, and her parents took Doug to live with them.

In 1950, Calvin finally returned to the mountains he loved so well, and under the G.I. Bill of Rights, he studied auto mechanics at the Mayo State Vocational School in Paintsville, Kentucky, graduating on July 31, 1953. A year or so after graduating, he went home to Morris Fork and went to work as a mechanic in a garage in Jackson. He did not return to the little church in Morris Fork, however. By this time, he'd married again and had a little daughter, Mary Sue.

In 1958, Calvin's beloved Granny died. Her body lies in the little graveyard high on a hillside overlooking the little valley community she loved and served so well. Her death was a crushing blow for Calvin, and a turning point in his life. His drinking problem worsened, and he and his second wife separated. She and Mary Sue went to live with her mother in Michigan, and Calvin went to Middletown, Ohio, where he tended bar in the 900 Club. It was there I met him for the first time.

Chapter 11

Booze in the Snow

When I met Calvin, his divorce wasn't final, and his wife was still living in Michigan with their little girl, Mary Sue. "I really love that child," Calvin told me one day with a deep sigh. "And I miss her so." He was overjoyed when his wife decided to move out west and asked him to take Mary Sue. She came to live with us before we left for Kentucky, just before the Middletown bar was closed.

From the first, Mary Sue and I didn't like each other very much. Although she was only five years old—a fair, blue-eyed little girl—she was jealous of me. I was too immature to cope with it, so I treated her coldly.

When the 900 Club closed, the three of us—Calvin, Mary Sue and I—drove to the bluegrass country in western Kentucky where Calvin went into business again with his cousin in another bar. It was, however, a short-lived partnership. There was a dispute over money, and they split. It left us—within days of the expected arrival of a baby—without a home or a roof over our heads.

"Let's go home to my mother," I suggested to

Calvin. "I'm sure she'll keep us for a while. At least until I have the baby." Mother and Daddy had sold the farm in Ridgeville—where I went to high school—and had moved to Waynesville. My mother was not at all happy to see us, but my kids were. Lynn, my lovely, green-eyed eleven-year-old, greeted me with a big hug and kiss. She was so excited, jumping up and down on her scrawny, thin legs. "Lynn, you're getting so tall!" I exclaimed, giving her an affectionate squeeze.

My three "all boy" boys were happy to see me, too. Tommy, the eldest, now eight years old, bounded around the living room causing quite a commotion. "Tommy, watch the lamp," Mother cautioned, trying to settle them down a bit. Even Kevin, usually shy and withdrawn—not as outgoing as the others—showed his affection, hanging on to me like he didn't want to ever let go.

I turned to my youngest, four-year-old Gregg. "Look," I said, pushing Mary Sue in his direction. "Here's a little playmate for you! Show her some of your toys and coloring books. She likes to color, don't you, Mary Sue?" The children were soon happily employed, and I had a chance to talk to my dear Daddy.

"The kids miss you," he said. "Kevin even sleeps with a pair of your old pajamas." I bit my lip to hold back the tears. "But we love them," he assured me.

Mother was cordial but somewhat aloof. She set us a sumptuous meal, but later in the kitchen where I went to help scrape the plates and clean up, she said candidly, "I think I can guess why you've come, Myrle." She looked at my full stomach. "You're due any day now, aren't you?"

I guess she thought I was bringing her home another

child to care for. But I wasn't. I planned to keep this baby. I didn't tell her that, but I did try to explain our predicament. "We need a place to stay for a few days, just until the baby is born. Then we're going back to Kentucky." And I tried to give her a little background on how our business had fallen through.

I couldn't believe she would turn me down, but she did. She was blunt and to the point. "No, I won't have you here. Not with Calvin. He's not your husband, and it's a bad influence for your own babies." And she added sternly, "I care about them, even if you don't."

I had too much pride to tell her I could go into labor at any moment. Too much pride to confess we had very little money to get a room anywhere. So I straightened my shoulders resolutely, put on a phony smile and walked out to the living room where Calvin and Daddy were visiting. We left soon after, amidst the disappointed clamor of the children and Daddy's polite but sincere, "Come back soon, Myrle."

In the car we had an old mattress we'd brought with us. We'd found it in a pile of junk in back of the bar where we'd lived in Kentucky. It came in handy now. "We'll find a place near Middletown, close to the hospital, and camp out," Calvin said. "Besides, it's warm outside. Thank goodness we're in the middle of summer!" He tried to keep his conversation bright, but I sensed he was on edge, as I was. "I just don't understand," he muttered as we drove down the country road, "how your mother could send you out into the night, knowing you could have a baby at any time."

"I don't think she realized how soon the baby is due," I defended. "Besides, she probably thinks we can make alternate plans."

Calvin picked a spot halfway between Ridgeville and Middletown. We knew of a sandbar there because so many spring and early summer evenings we'd sat along the banks of the creek, listening to the water gurgling along, sipping beer and sharing life's griefs. Most of, which we brought upon ourselves, but, of course, we never acknowledged that.

We bedded down on the sandbar; Mary Sue fell asleep, leaving Calvin and me awake to stare up into the starry sky. As we listened to the frogs and the crickets, I went into labor. Calvin rushed me to the hospital where an hour later, I delivered a darling baby boy. His hair was coal black. We named him Calvin, Jr., and he was born July 30, 1961.

Two days later, we were on our way to Kentucky where Calvin's father and stepmother received us kindly, even letting us stay with them in their very tiny house—under very cramped conditions—until we found our own place.

When Calvin found a job as a mechanic at a local garage, we rented a little four-room shack by the river in Quicksand, Kentucky, about twenty-eight miles from Morris Fork. It had no plumbing and it was, to say the least, rustic. But the rent was only $20 a month, so we busied ourselves fixing it up—painting and putting in window panes. Calvin had to chop wood for the fireplace, which was our only source of heat. Our water was drawn by bucket from an outside well—but we were happier than either of us had been for a long time.

In the river back of our cabin, we kept a trotline and had fish whenever we wanted it. Because the river flooded every spring, the house was on stilts, and we had ground squirrels living beneath us. Across the road, a family of flying squirrels lived in a birdhouse up in a tree. Beautiful little green lizards with bright blue tails scampered back and forth across our yard. Once, just after I had finished picking two buckets full of blackberries, a neighbor boy killed a rattlesnake just up the road from where I had been picking. I lost all enthusiasm, after that, for picking blackberries.

When I lived in Quicksand, I enjoyed getting acquainted with my neighbors. One lady, Hilda taught me how to quilt. Another one taught me how to make cornbread and biscuits. I learned how to can, too. Although it only lasted a short time, it was refreshing to know decent people, not just bar flies, thieves and prostitutes. And it meant so much to me that good people liked me. "They wouldn't like me if they knew my past," I told Calvin one night when he came home from the garage. He only laughed. He knew I was very careful not to let any of these mountain women know what I really was.

Since Breathitt county where we lived was "dry," Calvin and I didn't drink as much as before. But every payday we'd buy booze with money that should have gone for things we really needed. On Labor Day that year, some of the old gang from Ohio found out where we lived and drove down with a car full of liquor and a tobacco can stuffed with marijuana. It was my first introduction to "grass." When I disappeared, Calvin came searching for me and found me sitting all alone by the river with the whole can of marijuana. I was rolling my own "joints" and smoking one after another. It left me numb. I liked the feeling it gave me. It put me in a blissful, fake world. Reality was no more. Problems? I didn't have any when I smoked pot that Labor Day weekend in Kentucky.

But the numbness didn't last and reality returned. At Christmas time I was miserably homesick for my children back in Ohio. "Calvin, I've got to see my kids. I've never missed being with them at Christmas."

"Too bad you won't be there this Christmas," was his terse reply.

"You don't mean that," I lashed back at him.

"Yes, I do. You know we can't afford for you to make a trip to Ohio now."

But I couldn't believe he wouldn't let me go. Even when I was hanging out in the bars, I always managed to get to Mother's and Daddy's for Christmas. And I'm going *this* Christmas, I promised myself. And told Calvin as much.

"I said you're not going, and you're not going!" was his final word on the subject.

We had a heated argument until I ran weeping from my warm house into the snow and the darkness of a winter's night. "Don't be stupid!" he yelled after me. But he didn't follow. Instead, he sent Mary Sue, bundled warmly against the icy wind, out to look for me. She found me at a neighbor's house down the road where I'd gone, trudging through the snow, to phone my children in Ohio. Hearing their sweet child voices over the wire only made matters worse and strengthened my excuse to get drunk. Which I did as soon as I returned home with Mary Sue.

Calvin had some "moonshine" he was saving. I took it and walked coatless again into the snowy night. It was very cold, but I didn't feel the chill. Mary Sue found me and led me back into the house where Calvin and I continued our battle until he threw a bowl of beans at me. He missed, and they went all over the wall and ceiling. I walked into the bedroom and passed out across the bed.

Chapter 12

Kidnaped!

A few months after Calvin and I moved into our little mountain cabin in Kentucky, we had a visit from Calvin's old friend, Mort, and his girlfriend, Connie.

"I'm wanted now by the F.B.I.," Mort told us. "Can you beat that?" And he laughed. They used our home as a hideout for several weeks and all I heard was, "It's so easy to make money." "It's so wonderful to have pretty clothes and drive big cars." Mort would wear flashy diamonds and always drove a Cadillac.

I was tempted by what they offered. "You sure are missing a lot of fun living back here in the sticks," Mort said one day. And he began describing one of his rackets. He used knockout drops to put people to sleep and then he robbed them. "It's a piece of cake," he said.

"Why don't we travel together for a while?" Mort enticed. "We'll show you the ropes and how you can make a lot of money."

After a few weeks of constant badgering, Calvin finally agreed to join their con games. We left Mary Sue with some of the relatives and took Calvin, Jr., with us. The crime spree didn't last long. Calvin and I were a couple of drunks, so we really didn't like stealing money from other drunks. We left Calvin, Jr., with Mort and Connie in St. Louis, Missouri, and went on down to New Orleans, Louisiana. We were looking for a new life, thinking perhaps we could get a fresh start. Calvin was looking for a job.

In early November, we took a room in a motel there and ate our meals in a diner about two blocks down the highway. Among the regular customers in this eating place was a small, slightly-built man who always came over and sat with us. He introduced himself as Al and said he was an airplane mechanic working out at the airport. He and Calvin talked a lot about mechanics, and he brought us up-to-date on local happenings. One story he told us about concerned a brutal murder that had occurred about a week before we arrived in New Orleans. "One of the airline hostesses was killed with a shotgun in her own apartment," he said. "They found her body in the bathtub, fully clothed." It made me shudder when he told us about it.

On our third day in New Orleans, I left Calvin at the motel about nine o'clock in the morning and walked down to the diner to see about getting a job as a waitress. Al was sitting at the counter drinking a cup of coffee. I sat down beside him and told him why I was there. He asked where Calvin was. "He's back at the motel," I answered.

"The reason I asked," he explained, "is because I heard of a job Calvin could get at the airport. It pays so well, it wouldn't be necessary for you to work at all."

"That's great!" I said, getting fluttery over the prospects of a steady income.

"Let's go find Calvin right away!" He jumped up

and offered, "I'll drive you back to the motel to get him."

Believing this to be more important than seeing about a job for myself, I agreed. As we pulled out of the parking lot in his car, Al turned left—away from the motel—and roared down the highway at high speeds. When I begged him to turn around, or at least slow down, he laughed at me and said cruelly, "Shut up!"

After a few miles of this hair-raising ride, we came to an open drawbridge and had to stop. Pushing against the door on my side, I tried to jump out, but Al grabbed my arm and I couldn't jerk free. I screamed for help and waved my other arm wildly, trying to attract people in the cars behind us. But my efforts only drew blank stares. They must have concluded we were having a lovers' quarrel, or a marital disagreement. No one wanted to get involved. As soon as the bridge was closed, Al jerked the car into motion, and I had no choice but to stay in it. Trying to drive and hold my arm at the same time, he sideswiped a passing car, but that didn't slow him down one little bit.

At last he turned the car into a driveway and pulled up to the back door. Shoving me out of the car and into the house, he forced me into the bathroom. The house, I noticed, was empty. "Take off your shoes and get into the tub with your clothes on!" He glared at me. Suddenly, all the pieces fit, and I knew *he* had murdered that airline hostess!

Anxiously, I looked around for a way to get out of the house. My chance came when Al left me momentarily to get something out of his car. I could hear him lift the trunk. I made a mad lunge for the front door, and praying it wouldn't be locked, gave it a jerk. It opened—

just in time! I could hear Al's footsteps and his heavy breathing behind me, as he closed the gap between us.

Heedless of the stones that cut and bruised my bare feet, I ran toward the next house—about a block away—without daring to look back. Miraculously, the door opened almost immediately when I banged on it with both fists, and I pushed my way in past the two young girls who lived there and who were just starting out on their way to work. Slamming the door behind me and gasping for breath, I shouted, "Lock the door! Call the police!"

The detectives who arrived moments later took me back to the house where I had so narrowly escaped death. It was locked, and Al was gone. Locating the landlord, they got the key, opened the door, and found my purse and shoes in the bathroom. Then they drove me back to the diner where it had all started. There, in the parking lot, was the car that had earlier been my prison. The police found Al inside the diner and, in the trunk of his car, a double-barreled shotgun. Recognizing how close I'd come to being murdered, I went into shock and began to shake uncontrollably.

After that traumatic experience, we lost our taste for New Orleans. Calvin and I headed back to Ohio, arriving in time to spend Christmas at my parents' home. And on Christmas Eve, I knelt down and thanked God for saving my life. "God, I'm so sorry for the way I've been living. I promise—since You've spared my life—I'll try to do better."

Chapter 13

A Faltering Step

After the holidays, Calvin got a good job as a mechanic in a Dayton service station. We brought Mary Sue and Calvin, Jr., home and we all moved to a suburb of Dayton where we rented a three-room chicken house with a slab floor. It was located on the back of our landlord's apple orchard. He drank booze morning, noon and night, so we felt at home with him. There weren't too many places available for people who drank like we did, and so we were satisfied.

In the early spring the apple trees bloomed and for a while it was like living in a fairyland of glorious color and fragrance. Most of the time, however, I was too drunk to appreciate the beauty of my surroundings. Calvin would bring beer in after work, and I'd drink all day and try to act sober when he got home. But I never fooled him, and we ended up feuding. Weekend after weekend, both of us existed in a drunken indifference. We "swore off" alcohol with every hangover—but as soon as Calvin got another paycheck, we'd rush out and buy more.

Next to liquor, my best escape from reality was television. One night in September, 1963, I happened to turn to a channel that was carrying the Billy Graham Crusade from the Los Angeles Coliseum. "Jesus Christ, the Son of God, died to take away your sins forever!" Dr. Graham said.

I'd never heard such a statement. Not from any human being had I ever heard the things Billy Graham told the audience that night. It was simple, yet profound. And I felt moved when thousands from all over that massive stadium walked forward to the center field to open their hearts and lives to Jesus' leadership.

I began to weep with many of them, and— embarrassed for my family to see me—I stepped outside into the late summer evening. There, by an apple tree in the middle of the orchard, I dropped to my knees and cried out to God. "Oh, God! Be merciful to me, a sinner. Forgive me. I'm such a miserable person. Please, Lord Jesus, come into my heart."

I remember the happiness I felt because Someone really loved me enough to die for me. Now I understood, for the first time, the significance of Christ's death on the cross. It was for *me!* "All my sins are gone—gone forever!" And I stood to my feet feeling cleaner than I'd ever felt in my whole life.

For a few months, I *was* a "new creature" in Christ Jesus (2 Corinthians 5:17). I took Mary Sue and Calvin, Jr., to church, stopped drinking and put all my determination into being a "good" Christian. For me, that meant: quit cussing, smoking and drinking, and go to church. Of course, the more important things like daily prayer and Bible study and fellowship with God's people, other than Sunday morning, were ignored. I just wasn't aware that I was supposed to do these things.

Then I began listening to the voice of Satan—that

negative suggestion he whispers in the ear of all newborn babes in Christ. "You're not *really* saved. Look at your sinful life! And to top it off, you're still living with Calvin out of wedlock."

I loved Calvin and didn't want to leave him. But it did begin to bother me that we weren't married. I broached the subject one morning while the eggs were frying on the stove. "Calvin, can we get married soon?"

He was sitting at the kitchen table, reading the early morning paper and drinking a beer. He laughed. "What in the world brought that on all of a sudden?" he asked. And then his face became more serious. "Myrle, you know why we can't. You know I would have married you long ago if I could have."

I believed him because I knew he really loved me. Rhoda, his ex-wife, had gone to Arizona. He was afraid that if he sued her for a divorce, she might contest it and maybe he'd lose custody of Mary Sue. Since we didn't have money for a lawyer, we didn't know what to do about the situation. We also knew she didn't have any money either and was living with an alcoholic. We didn't even know her address.

That morning, after Calvin went to work and Mary Sue went to school, I got Calvin, Jr., engrossed in the pages of a large picture book so I could enjoy a second cup of hot tea. I carried it into the living room and sat down on a big chair, trying to plot my way through this dilemma.

"There's no way out," I erroneously concluded. "Jesus isn't working for me." I couldn't face that "fact," so I returned to the kitchen, opened the refrigerator, reached for a can of cold beer and guzzled down the foaming gold liquid. I wiped my lips with the back of my hand. "You've really done it now, Myrle," I said outloud. "You've turned your back on Jesus . . . like a dog going back to its vomit."

Futile days of fear and frustration followed. There were terrifying nights when I'd wake up in a cold sweat with the knowledge, "I walked away from God!" It hit me again and again like the physical blows of Calvin's drunken beatings. "I have sinned so much that God is through with me forever," I told myself. "Being an alcoholic won't make my punishment any worse."

This kind of reasoning took me into a living hell on earth. "I'm just a walking dead person, floundering around with a lot of other dead people." I had no hope for the future and I hated to see the sun come up in the morning. But God wasn't finished with me yet.

Chapter 14

God Is Bigger Than Cancer

Just a few short months later, God intervened once again in my life in a dramatic way. He allowed me to go through an abysmal experience that set me back on my heels and made me think in terms of eternity.

During a doctor's appointment in Waynesville, I had a pap smear. I paid cash for the office visit and left, not realizing I'd left no address or phone number where they could reach me concerning the report. When the report came back that I had an advanced case of cervical cancer, the doctor tried frantically to locate me. But he had no clues as to where or how to find me.

One day, about a month later, I went back to Waynesville. My Daddy operated a laundromat there so, with Calvin, Jr., still a babe in arms, and six-year-old Mary Sue, I went to wash clothes. As Mary Sue opened the laundromat door, she hooked her thumb in the catch of the door. It ripped her thumb wide open. She screamed, and I saw blood gushing everywhere. I knew she had to have stitches right then. Since I had gone to the doctor the month before, I knew where to go. His office was just about a block away. That's where I rushed Mary Sue.

When we burst into his office and he was summoned by the nurse, he looked at me and said animatedly, "Mrs. Morris, (I had let on that Calvin and I were married), I've been trying to find you for more than a month!" I didn't have the faintest inkling of what he was talking about. "I had no address for you," he continued. Then looking quickly at my face and Mary Sue's thumb, he said, "Never mind that now. Let's fix the little girl's thumb. I'll talk to you later."

He treated Mary Sue, and I sent her back to the laundromat. The doctor took me into his private office, sat me down in a big chair, and said, "Mrs. Morris, I only wish I'd known it was your father who ran the laundry down the street. I'd have been able to get to you sooner. As it was, I just had no idea how to reach you. The reason I tried to contact you is because your pap smear report came back positive."

I wasn't too impressed, because I didn't understand the ramifications of a pap smear. He went on, "Mrs. Morris, I'm terribly sorry, but you have cancer of the cervix. And it's a very serious condition. I insist that you go into the hospital tomorrow morning."

I was scared to death. I was so absolutely overwhelmed with fright and the knowledge that I was going to die that I didn't know what to do. Somehow, I got out of his office and back to the laundromat and told Daddy. I saw his chin quiver and his eyes fill with tears. When he did that I started to sob and couldn't quit. I wept my way home and waited for Calvin to come home from work. As soon as he walked in the front door, I ran to him and held him close. "I have cancer of the cervix, Calvin," I told him. "And I just know I'm going to die," and I

96

dissolved into tears again.

Calvin, who experiences so many profound emotions deep inside, said nothing. He held me for a while and dried my tears. Then he walked outside and began hoeing the garden. I knew then that he was beside himself with worry; this was his behavior whenever he was emotionally upset. He'd go off by himself and work real hard, thinking all the time, trying to work out the puzzle pieces in his mind.

The next day I entered the Grandview Hospital in Dayton. I was there off and on for about two-and-one-half months. My doctor was Dr. John E. Thomas of Waynesville, Ohio. I was too far advanced for an operation, but they put me in the hospital for radiation therapy. "I can't offer you much hope," my doctor said, as gently as he could. "We'll do everything medically possible to lengthen your life."

When he said that, I just flipped out. That's the only way I can explain my reaction. I couldn't handle it. Again and again, between the thirty or more chemotherapy treatments and two cervical radium implants, I'd run away from home. Usually I'd go to Middletown to the same old bars where I used to go. Calvin knew where to find me most of the time, and he'd bring me back home. In the course of time, I had two nervous breakdowns. Sometimes I couldn't even tell him where I'd been. I'd find myself on the street and would call him from a phone booth.

I was running scared; unable to face my illness, trying with all my being to escape cancer as I had tried to flee all my life from every other difficulty. Every time I left home, I never told Mary Sue or Calvin where I was going. I just left, leaving them to look after little Calvin,

Jr., and do the housework. Sometimes Calvin knew where I was; sometimes he didn't. On occasion I would telephone before returning. Mary Sue normally answered the telephone. "Is Daddy mad?" I'd ask her. Whether he was or not, I went home. Both of them would give me a cold shoulder and the silent treatment. Calvin was angry at me for running away, and when I'd get home, he'd start drinking, ending up whipping me for leaving.

One day, while I was in the hospital for a radium implant, a Christian woman shared the room with me. While I was being turned every few hours like a barbecuing chicken, I observed this dark-haired woman with the sweet face. Her husband, a big guy, visited her regularly and always said hello to me. They talked a lot about Jesus and I listened when they did.

During one afternoon visit, this Christian lady got up, put on her bath robe and stepped out the door with her husband. I thought they were going for a walk. But instead, I found out later, they went next door to pray for a man with stomach cancer. She came back, slipped quietly into bed, gave me a bright smile, but said nothing about where she'd been.

The implant—which was not a cure but just to keep the cancer from spreading—took three days, and during that time the man next door who had stomach cancer was marvelously healed. I never met him personally, but I didn't have to. He caused such a furor that I heard of nothing else the entire time I was there. Nurses, orderlies, doctors—everyone—were discussing him. The man had raised quite a commotion.

The whole place was abuzz. The news traveled through the hospital like a prairie wind whipping up a dust storm. "There's this nut in here who says, 'Praise the Lord! I know I'm healed by the hand of Almighty God!' Can you imagine that?"

Or, "He says he's not going to be operated on!"

"He wants his clothes so he can go home!"

"He's crazy!"

And so it went—the patients receiving a play-by-play account through word-of-mouth—until he agreed to take one more X-ray to prove he'd been healed of cancer. They took their X-ray and found, as he had said, no trace of the disease. It was quite a story, and a miracle which apparently turned the doctors inside out. I realized the Lord was trying to give me a message. And I did appreciate what He had done for this man. But could He do it for me?

One day the X-ray technician came into the room to check my condition. He knew I was distraught and knew I'd run away many times because I was so frightened. He held my hand that day and tried to comfort me, like a mother cooing over a hurt child. "This isn't going to hurt," he said, "just try to relax. Everything is going to be all right."

As he spoke to me, a Bible story from my childhood appeared vividly in my mind. It was the New Testament story of the woman with the issue of blood who was healed when she touched the hem of Christ's garment (Matthew 9:20).

"Lord, let me touch You," I began to pray silently. I didn't think He would heal me just because I asked Him, knowing what a sinner I was, but He might heal me for the sake of Calvin, Jr., and Mary Sue and my other children living with my parents. I tried to con Him and bargain with Him.

"Lord, I know You love my kids. They've never done anything wrong. Please let me live to see them grown, and let me live to raise little Calvin and Mary Sue; they need a mother, even if I am a miserable one. If You let me live, I promise I'll get down to business with God."

Suddenly, I knew I had touched the Lord, just like the sick woman in the New Testament. A conviction spread throughout my being, "God has healed me!" In His love, the Lord gave me supernatural faith to believe that He had touched me right then, even while the technician was talking to me. And I began telling everyone, "Jesus has healed me!"

The technician smiled with eyes full of pity. And my doctor, when he heard, decided to humor me along. "Of course you're healed, Myrle. You're going to be all right." I guess everyone thought I'd had another nervous breakdown. Besides that, healing of my body didn't change my life too much. I'd become addicted to drugs in the hospital. They'd given me a little red pill they referred to as "happy pills." They were anti-depressants or "uppers." When I was flying too high with these, they gave me a depressant to bring me down a little. I became used to these pills and between hospital visits, I'd continue taking them. That's how I got hooked.

I kept regular appointments with Dr. Thomas, and he counseled and advised me, "Myrle, you have to give up drinking and taking dope! Don't you know you're killing yourself?" And he tried to pound into my mind every reason he could think of to persuade me to keep sober and live straight. But I was an emotional mess, and we both knew it. There wasn't much anyone could do for me.

On every examination after I confessed my healing, the doctors found less and less cancer. Until finally there was no trace of it whatsoever! That was fourteen years ago. Dr. Thomas says, "Myrle, you're a walking miracle." Well, I really was. At least physically. But my heart wasn't a bit changed.

God was so merciful! Physically, He made me whole. And He wanted to give me a new life, too. But I just didn't understand that yet.

Besides alcohol, I continued to crave the drugs I'd been using in the hospital. I was already hanging around bars again, and now I started increasing the drugs, too. The truth was, I didn't want to sober up, so I "popped" anything and everything I could get my hands on. I took handfuls of amphetamines "uppers." Whatever I was offered, I swallowed down with my drinks. By God's mercy *only* I didn't get into heroin. Not because I didn't want to, but because I never met anyone in the bars where I frequented who was pushing it. And it was only by God's grace that I didn't die of poisoning, because mixing drugs and liquor can be a lethal combination.

Sometimes I stayed away from home days on end. Many times I took off for a month. There were times I was so sick I could hardly walk, and I frequently went blind for periods of twenty-four hours. The only person I saw fairly regularly, besides Calvin and the children, was my doctor. He kept close tabs on my condition. "You're still free of cancer," he'd say with a broad smile. But there was concern in his eyes, too.

"Myrle, I know you're living a rotten existence. Please pay attention to what I tell you. You've got to straighten yourself out, or you're going to kill yourself with alcohol and drugs!" I know I exasperated him.

My doctor knew a lot about me because I was very frank with him about myself. I would quit drinking a few hours before each of my scheduled appointments. He didn't understand how I'd been healed of cancer and was now trying to kill myself with booze and dope. "I expect to receive a phone call at any hour telling me you've been found dead. Why do you abuse yourself so?"

How could I answer him? I couldn't explain it myself. By then I'd gotten so I'd sit on a barstool from morning until closing time, associating with ex-cons who robbed for a living. I bought my clothes in a Good Will Store and took baths in tavern restrooms. I completely gave up. There was nothing I valued in life.

Several years had passed and Calvin had saved enough money to hire a lawyer who advised him to go ahead with a divorce from Rhoda. There was no contest. Rhoda didn't even appear in court. "Do you think it will help you if I marry you?" Calvin asked. There was a tinge of humor in his voice, but a deep wistfulness, too. "Will it change you?"

"I don't know," I threw back at him. "Will it change *you*?"

We were married on his birthday, Christmas Eve, by a justice of the peace. Even though my relationship with my sister, Jean, had never grown any closer since we were kids, I still loved her very much, so she and her boyfriend were our witnesses.

But a wedding ceremony didn't help, as nice as it was. It didn't keep me out of Middletown bars, because I still hadn't found that depth of love that I was looking for.

Chapter 15

The Day of My Death

Soon after Calvin and I were married we moved from our chicken house to a large country house near my teenage stomping grounds in Ridgeville. After we moved, we sent Mary Sue and Calvin, Jr., to the little Ridgeville community church that I had attended as a teenager. I wanted everyone in the church to believe that Calvin and I were good parents. Of course, we both knew we weren't, but I tried to play the role when I saw church people. I knew everyone so well in Ridgeville, and they knew me, too. One of them, a little Christian neighbor, prayed for me every day for more than a year. She'd go to church and ask the people there to pray for me, too. I didn't know about this until much later. They were such faithful, loving people.

The last time I left home for any period of time, I went with a girl and her boyfriend to California in the summer of 1968. I guess I was running away again. I had been so depressed since my Daddy died the spring of that same year. He had died so suddenly, so unexpectedly. It was a big jolt for me. Jean phoned and said, tearfully, "Daddy's dying." I rushed to him, but I arrived too late. He was lying on the couch; he had already taken his last breath.

"Daddy," I cried, and buried my face in his still-warm chest, my whole body literally racked with sobs. I wanted to tell him, before he passed away, how sorry I was for the many times I'd hurt him. Now he couldn't hear my plea. "Daddy! Daddy! I'm so sorry! I'm so sorry!"

There was no fulfillment in California. I was just as empty there as I was wherever I went. After arriving in Los Angeles, and staying with some friends for three weeks, I telephoned Calvin. "Can you send me money for an airplane ticket?" I begged.

"How do I know you won't spend it on liquor?" he responded.

"Oh, Calvin, I'm so miserable and unhappy." I choked back the tears and tried to swallow the lump in my throat.

"Myrle, I'll send you the money. I love you, Honey, and miss you. And we need you here."

So he wired me the airline fare; I gave my car away and flew home in September. But when I got off the plane, nothing had changed. Everything was the same. It was at this point I began to plan for my whole family's death and I wrote the suicide letter. I hated myself and what I was. I wanted to die. I had finally come to the end of the line and knew I couldn't hack it any longer. Since I had decided to defer my death plans until after Christmas, I had a couple of months to calculate every detail concerning the day of my death.

That Christmas Eve in 1968, Calvin and I were sitting in a Lebanon bar eating steak and drinking beer, celebrating our first wedding anniversary. A neighbor lady from Ridgeville—a faithful churchgoer—walked past the big front window of the bar. I sank down into the cushions of the booth, hoping she didn't see me.

"If you feel ashamed," Calvin commented with a look of disgust, "you shouldn't be in here."

I knew that lady was a Christian and I really thought I had them all fooled in Ridgeville by sending my kids to Sunday school. What a dummy I was!

New Year's Eve was spent drinking as usual, but this time I was careful not to get drunk. I wanted to be alert for the next day and didn't want to botch things up. It was all over but the crying—and boy, would everyone shed tears over the way they'd treated me!

I slept on the couch all night and awoke very early. I tried to get up, but found it impossible. I felt so weak, helpless and sick. Soon after I opened my eyes, Mary Sue and Calvin, Jr., came into the living room playing with their new Christmas toys, laughing and giggling together. Still, I was unable to get up. About an hour later, Calvin came in, opened a beer and took his seat in front of the television set, to remain there for the rest of the day.

As I lay on the couch and looked at the children, God began dealing with me through the power of the Holy Spirit. First, He brought to my mind the times He had intervened to spare my little boy's life. *Do you remember when Calvin, Jr., fell off a cliff in the mountains of Kentucky?* He asked. *"Remember how he rolled down a steep slope through glass, rocks and tin cans?"*

"Yes," I said to myself. "When I got to him, he was fine. Not a scratch on him."

"And what about the other time," the Lord

continued, *"when you were driving down that freeway forty miles an hour and Calvin, Jr., tumbled out the door?"*

The memory made me wince. I had slammed on the brakes, jumped out of the car and run back to him. It was like a nightmare. There he stood, with arms outstretched to me, right in the path of a fast-moving automobile. Moving with superhuman strength and speed, I snatched him out of death's way just in time.

"Who helped you do that?" the Lord prompted.

"Was it You, Lord?" I asked. And instinctively, I knew the answer.

Still another incident came to mind. That was the time in Kentucky when Calvin, Jr., began having convulsions after eating a tomato sprayed with a pesticide containing lead. He almost died before we could get him to the nearest hospital fifty miles away. Yes, I remembered those twisting mountain roads.

"You and Calvin both prayed then as you stood looking out the window in his hospital room. I healed your baby and gave him back to you."

"Oh, Lord," and I began to weep. Tears trickled down my cheeks as I lay there, looking at that same little boy playing on the floor in front of me. How could I entertain thoughts of snuffing out a life God had so tenderly protected three times within seven years?

Then the Lord began to deal with me about Mary Sue as I thought of my cruel indifference to this precious little girl. She was a teenager now, having just passed her thirteenth birthday on December 8th.

"You have withheld your love and affection from this child," the Lord admonished.

Yes, it was true. I had treated Mary Sue like a slave. I

had always resented her because I had to look after someone else's daughter when I couldn't raise my own. Lynn, now eighteen years old—my firstborn, my beautiful little girl—was still with Mother in Waynesville. Yes, I hated Mary Sue because she was not my Lynn. Looking at her now, a deep sympathy for her enveloped me. I felt genuine sorrow for the first time over my tawdry treatment of her. "I want to give her a better life," I cried within myself. "Oh, God! Oh, God, what have I done to her? And what am I about to do? If only I could make it all up to her!"

"You can, Myrle. You can." Again there was that inaudible, yet definite Voice deep within, talking to me. *"You don't have to go through with your death plans. I can change you, Myrle. Trust Me! Give Me a chance to help you."*

"Oh, God!" I cried. "Can you really do something with a loathsome person like me? And can You forgive me for all those times I've lied to You before? If You can, please change me from the inside out. I mean business this time!"

The rest of the day I reveled in the wonderful, healing love of Jesus, allowing it to permeate my being. When I closed my eyes, I could almost feel His arms around me. Here was the love I'd been searching for so long—the security I had needed all my life. How wonderful! How very wonderful!

I found the Bible was true. "Whoever comes to me I will never drive away" (John 6:37 *NIV*). And "In the same way, count yourselves dead to sin but alive to God in Christ Jesus. Therefore, do not let sin reign in your mortal body so that you obey its evil desires. Do not offer the parts of your body to sin, as instruments of wickedness, but rather offer yourselves to God, as those who have returned from death to life; and offer the parts of your body to him as instruments of righteousness. For sin shall not be your master, because you are not under law, but under grace" (Romans 6:11-14 *NIV*).

The Sunday following New Year's Day, 1969, I got up early and went to the Ridgeville church with my kids. I fully expected the congregation to laugh me out the door. Instead, everyone shook my hand and seemed sincerely glad to have me with them in the house of God. I'll always appreciate their love.

About two months later, I stood up in that church and told them what God had done for me. "I confess Jesus Christ as my personal Savior," I said. I was so frightened my knees were knocking together, but I was determined to go the whole route. And public confession of salvation was part of it.

Just before I went into the church that evening, I saw the pastor's wife, Jean Shelton, a lovely, well-groomed Christian lady. She knew I was scheduled to give my testimony that evening, and she squeezed my hand as she passed by me. But I wouldn't let her go. "I'm scared to death," I told her. Mrs. Shelton smiled kindly and reminded me of a verse of scripture, "I can do everything through him who gives me strength" (Philippians 4:13 *NIV*).

From the moment I stood up that night in church, I have been able to testify concerning my faith in Jesus Christ.

Chapter 16

Living Water

There was no longer any heaviness in my heart. In fact, I was full of joy most of the time. I had tasted the dregs of the earth, and now I was drinking at the Fountain of Living Water! I still had my problems, but I could take them in stride. Calvin still drank, but Jesus had given me real hope.

One night after choir practice, I was sharing with one of my sisters in Christ. "The Lord really helped me through the strain of this week," I said. Calvin had been drinking so heavily, but, as I told this Christian friend, "Jesus brought me through."

She smiled and said, "Yes, I know. Jesus is enough to meet all our needs. He has done it all for us on the cross." She also explained that there is more: that Jesus is not only our Savior and Healer, but also our Baptizer into the Holy Spirit. I realized then she did have something I lacked—a peace and a power, combined with gentleness and compassion. When I talked with our pastor, Ray Shelton, and his wife, Jean, I noticed this same combination of peace, power and gentleness in them. When I was with them, I knew I had been close to the Lord.

I knew by now, too, that God is no respecter of persons, and that whatever He has given His other children, He would give me. I also realized I wanted all He had for me! I went to talk to Pastor Shelton about it. He was in his late forties, a dark-haired, black-eyed man who walked straight and erect. He knew exactly what I needed and how to help me. He explained, "There is another vital step in a Christian's life, Myrle, that he needs to take." He gave me some scriptures to study, and set a date for me to come to his office in the church.

Reading the scriptures, I learned about the mighty Holy Spirit. I found out that He is a Person—the third Person in the Trinity (God the Father, God the Son, and God the Holy Spirit). I read that the Holy Spirit will impart power to men (Luke 24:49); that He will teach all things (John 14:26); that He bears witness that we are God's children (Romans 8:16). He works miracles through believers (Acts 5:15-16); and strengthens the inner man (Ephesians 3:16). I read in the second chapter of Acts about the Holy Spirit's descending on the apostles on the day of Pentecost, as they waited in the upper room. The thrill of that wonderful moment became so real to me that I fully expected the rushing wind and the cloven tongues like fire to be part of my experience. I couldn't *wait* until my appointment with Pastor Shelton!

The day finally came—and when I went into his office, I was surprised to see that the windows were closed. I thought, "Wow! They must have to replace a lot of glass when that rushing wind comes in!"

When Pastor Shelton and his wife prayed with me, I was shocked that it was so quiet and peaceful. The

110

windows didn't break, and the building didn't quake! Pastor Shelton told me to relax and just praise the Lord. As I began praising Him in English, I could almost feel the presence of Jesus. Then I stopped speaking—and a word I didn't know came into my mind. After saying this word several times and thanking the Lord for my heavenly language, I got up off my knees, shook hands with the pastor and his wife, and left the church.

As I was getting into my car, I suddenly felt a tremendous surge of joy. It swept through my being like a mighty rushing wind! It was joy so great I felt as if I'd burst! It seemed God was saying, "You have received; now rejoice!" Throwing my head back, I laughed and prayed and praised God in a fluent language as the Spirit gave utterance (Acts 2:4). Never had I experienced such freedom and complete contentment! Now I could pray and have a direct channel to the Father, without any chance of Satan's interference. The Holy Spirit can say to the Father in a few words what it might take me forty years to say in English. It was a hotline to God!

The baptism in the Holy Spirit also brought me a wonderful peace and great power in prayer. Prayers that had not been answered before began to be resolved. Jesus became more real to me. He was very near—just a breath away—before; but now He was closer than hands or feet. The Holy Spirit came to glorify the Lord Jesus Christ (John 16:14), and this is what He did in my life. That day, He gave me more of my wonderful Savior and King, the beautiful Lord Jesus!

Chapter 17

Tommy, Another Gift

That spring of 1969, just a few months after my life was changed so miraculously, my daughter, Lynn, graduated from high school in Waynesville, Ohio. My oldest son, Tommy, sixteen years old, who had been living with his father in Detroit, came down to see his sister get her diploma. I met him at the bus station, and he could hardly believe his eyes when he saw how the Lord had transformed even my appearance. I told him I was happier than I'd ever been before.

"Mom, I know you've been praying for me," Tommy told me. "There were two times I almost got killed, but God spared my life." He also told me he had been going to church in Detroit with a neighbor boy who had been urging him to accept Christ as his Savior. How I rejoiced to know that God had been answering my prayers for my oldest boy while he was so many miles away!

The next day was Sunday, and Tommy went to Sunday school and church with me. Because I sang in the choir, he had to sit by himself in the congregation. When Pastor Shelton gave the altar call at the end of the service, I prayed that Tommy would go forward—but he remained in his pew. Dejectedly, I walked to the choir room to take off my robe. Then one of the church members came in to tell me that Tommy was standing by the altar, looking very sad. Throwing my robe to someone standing by, I hurried to him and asked, "Honey, would you like to pray and ask God to forgive you of your sins? Do you want to ask the Lord Jesus to come into your heart and be your Savior, too?"

He replied, "Yes, oh yes, I would, Mom!" My heart leaped with gladness! As we prayed together with tears falling heedlessly down our faces, Pastor Shelton and some of the church people came up and prayed with us. I'm sure the hosts of heaven rejoiced that morning as another lost sheep came home. What unspeakable joy filled my own heart!

On the way home from church, Tommy caused my cup of joy to overflow when he declared, "Mom, I don't want to go back to Detroit. I want to stay with you and Calvin."

A few weeks after he came to live with us, Tommy and I were both baptized in water—and soon afterwards Jesus baptized him in the Holy Spirit. On the Saturday before Mother's Day, he attended a prayer meeting at a church in Centerville, and there received his call from God to go into full-time service for Him. He woke me Sunday morning, on Mother's Day, to say, "Good morning, Mom! I couldn't wait to tell you what happened to me last night at church!" And he poured out his young heart, telling me his response to the altar call the night before.

A year or so after Tommy was saved, he and I attended a service conducted by Kenneth Copeland in

Dayton, Ohio. At the conclusion, God moved in a tremendous way and many people were saved and healed.

As we watched God moving among the people, Tommy turned to me and said, "Mom, I want that man to pray for my eye."

When Tommy was a little boy an injury left blood clots in his right eye. The accident left him with ten percent vision in that eye. He could not see through the cotton-like fiber left there by the blood clots. There were no glasses that could correct his problem, but the doctor had prescribed lenses that would rest his eyes as he read.

We went forward and Brother Copeland laid hands on Tommy and prayed a powerful prayer. In the loving kindness of God, the sight of his right eye was restored instantly!

A few years later, Tommy went away to college at Taylor University in Upland, Indiana. While he was there, he had the opportunity to play drums with a little group of college kids who ministered in a Christian coffee house each weekend. Once, Tommy wrote me a short note from school, and what was written on that page from a college boy only his own mother could appreciate. "Mom," he wrote, "I want to thank you for introducing me to Jesus. He sure has blessed us!"

And he sure had!

Chapter 18

Our Halfway Meeting

In the fall of 1969, Mary Sue went to Arizona to live with her mother. She was almost fifteen years old. Although our relationship had improved since I became a Christian, when her mother phoned and asked her to come and live with her, Mary Sue decided to go. Calvin and I talked it over and left the choice to Mary Sue.

After she left, Calvin missed her terribly, and drank even more heavily than before. He even threatened to kill me! I knew Satan was working double time in his life because he was so close to conversion. The more I prayed for him, the worse he got. I began feeling jumpy and nervous over Calvin's intimidation.

I didn't want a divorce. But, as I had explained to Calvin, "Unless you change your life and quit drinking, I'm going to leave you." And it wasn't too long after that that I decided to take Tommy and Calvin, Jr., and move to an apartment until he got his drinking under control. Much as I loved him, I felt I just couldn't stand living under such strain and impending danger any longer. I knew Calvin needed the Lord to

turn over a new leaf, but since he wasn't showing any
interest—that I could see—in going God's direction, I
chose to leave. When I told Calvin, he came back at me
with, "It doesn't say in the Bible you can leave me. You
ask your preacher!"

I knew what Jesus had to say about divorce (Matthew
5:32; Mark 10:2-12), but I also knew there were a few
scriptures on the way God wanted husbands to treat
their wives (Ephesians 5:25-28; Colossians 3:19). I
didn't argue with Calvin, however, since I knew from
experience that love was the only way to reach him. I
must admit I fell short there. I did not love Calvin and
submit to him as God expects us wives to do. I had so
much to learn myself and a lot of *self* to bring under
subjection to Jesus.

That evening, as the boys and I were leaving for
Wednesday night Bible study, Calvin called to me,
"Don't forget to ask your preacher if what I said isn't
right!"

After the meeting was over I did talk to Pastor
Shelton. He showed me that according to first
Corinthians, chapter seven, Calvin was right, that I
shouldn't leave my husband, even though he was an
unbeliever. Then Pastor Shelton and I prayed together,
asking God to lead me and show me what to say and do
when I went back home. After the prayer, the pastor was
very quiet for a few moments and then said, "Just tell
Calvin that you love him and don't want to leave. Then
ask him if he wouldn't please consider meeting you
halfway in the Lord—for Christ's sake, for his own
sake, and for the family's sake."

I was rather disappointed at this simple suggestion. I
guess I expected a hellfire-and-brimstone sermon to

deliver to Calvin! As I drove home, however, I asked God to help me say *just what He wanted* me to say. Tommy and Calvin, Jr., stayed in the car for a few minutes while I went inside and talked to Calvin.

As I opened the kitchen door, I saw my husband sitting at our old round table, just where he had been when we left for church. I was relieved to see he hadn't been drinking. As I closed the door, the first thing he said was, "Well, did you ask him? Wasn't I right?"

Standing there with my hand on the doorknob, I replied, "Yes, Honey, you are right about what God's Word says. He loves us all so very much. He doesn't want to see families separated. He wants us to love each other and to raise our children together as Christian parents. I don't want to argue with you, Honey. Won't you just . . . please . . . *meet me halfway in the Lord?*"

Calvin looked at me with a half-smirk and asked, "What do I have to do? Go over and talk to your preacher man?"

"That would be fine, Calvin, but you don't have to go anywhere; you can do it right where you are sitting. You can ask forgiveness and invite Jesus to come into your heart this very moment."

As I uttered those words, the power of God fell in that kitchen and I dropped to my knees right where I stood, with my hand still on the doorknob. I couldn't have stayed on my feet if I had wanted to. Burying my face in my Bible, I began to cry and praise the Lord silently. Just then, I heard a voice that I could hardly recognize, as Calvin cried out to God in anguished penitence, asking Him to forgive his sins. Then he invited Jesus to come into his heart, and promised to live for Him forever! I crawled over to Calvin and laid my head on his lap.

What ecstasy! Together we shed tears of joy and gave grateful thanks to God and to Jesus for the unspeakable gift of salvation. Then we went out to the car to tell the boys. Tommy grabbed Calvin and hugged him for the first time since he had been living with us. Our little one cried tears of joy, just as Calvin and I were doing, standing out in the barnyard in the quiet of the night.

That evening, for the first time in the years we had been sharing a bed, Calvin and I got down on our knees together before going to sleep. After prayer, Calvin said, "Myrle, it's like being in heaven already, isn't it?"

Sunday morning, Calvin went to church with us. I had asked Pastor Shelton if he thought it would be all right for me to sit with Calvin this Sunday in case he went forward to acknowledge Christ publicly. To my surprise, the pastor emphatically said, "No!" and then explained, "You do what you are supposed to do, and that's to sing in the choir. We have enough henpecked men already. When Calvin does decide to go forward, he doesn't need you to lead him by the hand."

It sounded like good advice, so I sat in the choir, barely able to keep my eyes off my new man. After the sermon, the pastor prayed, and before we could sing the invitation hymn, Calvin stepped out into the aisle and walked quickly forward. There, in the presence of the whole congregation, he knelt at the altar, and was prayed for and encouraged to live for the Lord.

I had always thought Calvin was a big man and the toughest I'd ever seen. At that moment, with tears running down his cheeks as he knelt before the Lord, he seemed bigger and stronger than ever before. I was so very proud of him, and that day I knew what it was to

120

love him in a way I'd never been able to before. In saving our souls, God also saved our marriage.

Everyone in the congregation came forward to shake Calvin's hand. Maggie, one of our dear friends from years back, had come to church that Sunday for the first time. I had always loved Maggie, who befriended me and Calvin when Calvin, Jr., was just a wee babe-in-arms. Her husband had worked with Calvin at the service station in Dayton, and the three of us had often gone on long drinking sprees together, while Maggie waited patiently for her man at home, even babysitting Mary Sue and Calvin, Jr. She never once let an angry word fly. She was a nondrinker and remained a true friend.

In time, Maggie really needed our friendship, too. Her husband just up and walked out on her, leaving her with a teenage boy and girl to raise. She sat sobbing in my kitchen one day, pouring out her grief and heartbreak, and I had nothing to say of comfort then. Not a shred of wisdom or spiritual advice. There was nothing we could do but pat her on the shoulder and say, "You'll be all right, Maggie. Just keep going. Something good will turn up. Somehow. Someway."

But now things were different. Now, we had a beautiful, life-changing love to share with her.

As Maggie came up to shake Calvin's hand, she was sniffling and wiping tears off her face. Calvin looked her squarely in the eyes and, putting his arm around her, said, "Please, Maggie, don't leave here without taking this step. Do it now!" As she hesitated for a moment, he pleaded, *"Won't* you?" She dropped to her knees right there and gave her life to Christ, too. What a day—what a marvelous day to remember always!

God knew all along, didn't He? Even though Calvin and I met under adverse circumstances, with no future and an ugly past, our heavenly Father knew how unhappy, how hardheaded we both were, and how much we needed Him. So with infinite love, patience, and longsuffering, He gently wooed us and won us to Himself. He gave us a new life together.

I turned in my Bible that afternoon when we returned home from church and read a beautiful verse of scripture that seemed to confirm the way I felt. "Yes, I have loved you with an everlasting love; therefore with loving-kindness have I drawn you and have continued My faithfulness to you" (Jeremiah 31:3 *AMP*).

Chapter 19

The Power of Submission

Calvin's new birth would probably have come about much earlier if I had fully understood what the Bible has to say about the husband-wife relationship, and if I had known how God honors submissiveness in a wife.

Ever since God created Adam and Eve, women have tried to be man's head instead of his helpmate. Eve sinned and then encouraged Adam to disobey God, too. I truly believe it is the Eve in all of us women that makes us want to lead our husbands—whether into sin or into salvation. God created Eve *for* Adam, and the Word of God is quite specific about the proper relationship of a wife to her husband.

"Wives, submit to your husbands as to the Lord. For the husband is the head of the wife as Christ is the head of the church, his body, of which he is the Savior. Now as the church submits to Christ, so also wives should submit to their husbands in everything" (Ephesians 5:22-24 *NIV*).

"Wives, in the same way be submissive to your husbands so that, if any of them do not believe the word, they may be won over without talk by the behavior of their wives, when they see the purity and reverence of your lives. Your beauty should not come from outward adornment, such as braided hair and the wearing of gold jewelry and fine clothes. Instead, it should be that of your inner self, the unfading beauty of a gentle and quiet spirit, which is of great worth in God's sight. For this is the way the holy women of the past who put their hope in God used to make themselves beautiful" (1 Peter 3:1-5 *NIV*).

When I first became a Christian and was trying to win my husband to the Lord, I was not submissive to him. I hadn't learned that this was what God wanted me to be. I preached to him constantly; I belittled him and condemned him for drinking; and I put myself on a pedestal, not realizing that only by the grace of God had I been saved. I actually drove Calvin away from the Lord by being so overzealous, self-righteous and demanding.

Shortly before Calvin's conversion, Pastor Shelton and his wife, Jean, began to teach me a little about the importance of submission, and I tried very hard to please God by pleasing my husband. It wasn't easy, but each time I submitted to Calvin with the *right attitude*, giving him all the love and understanding possible, God would honor my effort. Calvin told me, after he accepted Jesus, "The times I was under conviction the most were those times when you were so sweet to me. Even when I knew I didn't deserve anything, you would show me such kindness that I wanted to give in." But then—I know now—I'd blow the whole thing by losing my cool!

I still have a long way to go in learning how to wear "the unfading beauty of a gentle and quiet spirit"—for talking too much is one of my failings. But, with the help of the Holy Spirit, I'm going to keep striving to be more like the Master.

I also struggled in another area. I thought I loved everybody and had nothing against anyone. However, the Lord showed me that my motive for Bible study was—at least in part—really pride based on hate and resentment for the snubs I'd received in the past. He told me I had taken the sword of the Spirit (His Word) and used it against my Christian brothers and sisters, instead of against Satan. I had studied God's Word diligently, just so I would no longer feel inferior but would feel superior to other church people, and especially to Calvin. I praise God for showing me this lack of forgiveness, so I could repent and get rid of it.

One morning in a Sunday school class, He demonstrated to me what I was like. I noticed a woman sitting with her recently-saved husband. Watching her was like seeing myself in a mirror. She answered every question asked by the teacher, just loud enough for her husband to hear. Each time a scripture reference was given, she swiftly turned to it. She took notes on everything. Without even being aware of it, she was feeding her ego at the expense of her husband's self-respect. Just as I used to do before God revealed to me the real motive for my zeal in Bible study.

God gave me another insight a short time later. As I was using the vacuum cleaner, I suddenly found my shadow obscuring the part of the rug I was cleaning. Stepping aside, I could see the carpet more clearly. Just then, God spoke to me. *"That's right. Step aside and let Calvin be seen!"* It startled me so that I stopped my work and stood there quietly for a few minutes, meditating on what the Lord had revealed to me. We wives don't have to quit studying or praying; we just have to be careful we don't overshadow our husbands by taking the leadership in spiritual matters.

Calvin had great wells of wisdom I had never discovered until I stepped aside and took my rightful place as his helpmate. Since I have practiced being a submissive wife, he has taken his rightful place as spiritual leader in our home and is growing so fast spiritually it takes my breath away. It has been like watching a lovely flower bud and open.

Calvin's first Christian service activities included two things: he was nominated as a church trustee, and took over the leadership of a boys' group that met once a week in the Ridgeville church. He worked hard with that group called "The Brigade Boys" and pointed so many of them to the Savior.

I believe I have found true liberation in submissiveness to my Christian husband. "Where the Spirit of the Lord is, there is freedom" (2 Corinthians 3:17 NIV).

Chapter 20

Leaving the World Behind

Soon after I started walking with the Lord, He allowed me a difficult test. And I failed. I had just gotten a job in a tire recapping shop in Middletown when one morning, about fifteen minutes before my lunch break, a fellow from my old gang walked into the shop. I guess someone had told him where I was because he came to me immediately and said, "Myrle, I need some help in rolling a drunk. How about it?"

"No," I answered, "I'm a Christian now, and I'm not going to do those things any more."

He laughed and laughed. But he kept on talking until I gave in and went with him. In a matter of minutes, I was back on the job with my share of the money burning a hole in my pocket. As the afternoon wore on, that money seemed to get heavier and dirtier and hotter, until it was searing my flesh. Oh, how I wished I hadn't yielded to temptation! By the time I got off work that day, I was as jumpy and nervous as a cat.

I drove straight to the Ridgeville Church and found inside only the children's choir director, Sue, a kind Christian sister. Immediately, she sensed that something was amiss and asked, "Myrle, do you want us to go to the altar to pray?" Kneeling beside her there in the quietness of the sanctuary, I confessed my sin and asked God to forgive me. Tears of remorse and gratitude ran down my cheeks as I received His forgiveness again and allowed Him to wash my soul clean. Sue shared this scripture: "If we walk in the light, as he is in the light, we have fellowship with one another, and the blood of Jesus, his Son, purifies us from every sin" (1 John 1:7 NIV).

"Lord," I promised, "I'll never steal another thing the rest of my life." And with His help I've kept that promise. Times were pretty hard that year, too, and I lost my job at the tire company because they didn't have enough work. I then went to work as a field hand for some of the farmers in the area around Ridgeville. Hoeing vegetables all day raised big blisters on my hands, and I sometimes felt I couldn't lift that hoe another time; but then I would think of Jesus and remember what He had done for me, and I was given strength to keep going. I would rather work until I dropped than to hurt my Lord again by stealing.

In the spring, we faced another horrendous trial when Mort's old girlfriend, Connie, came to visit us with a new boyfriend, Jack. "We heard you were different," Connie said, "and we came to see for ourselves." Her mouth turned up in a "show-me" smile. In her eyes there lurked that same hunger I'd known for genuine love.

It was Wednesday night, so Connie and Jack went with us to Bible study. "I want to see what they're teaching you that makes you so happy," she explained on the way. At the altar call she raised her hand, but didn't go forward to receive Christ. "I felt such a tug on my heart to go to that altar," she told me on our return trip home. "I should have gone forward. From now on, nothing will go right for me."

It was such a sad statement, and as things turned out, in less than two weeks, it proved true. Connie was a pretty girl with a winning personality. She married when she was very young, but it didn't last. A series of romances ensued, and none of them proved permanent either. She seemed to be always attracted to the wrong type of men. They were either in trouble with the law, or running from it. Being with a rough crowd all the time hardened her, and she was bitter toward the world. I did think a lot of her, but I never fully trusted her.

Calvin and I had known Jack, too, for many years. We met him at the 900 Club and Calvin gave him a job as a "bouncer." He had just been released from the state penitentiary.

On the way home from church that Wednesday night, Connie shared, "Did you know Jack's mother is a Christian, and he knows the Bible backward and forward?"

He may have had a head knowledge of God's Word, but it sure wasn't lived out in his daily actions. He was handsome and intelligent, a neat dresser, but he had chosen a self-destructive path. Connie and Jack were both alcoholics and hooked on drugs.

A few weeks after they visited us, I was driving home from my mother's house in Waynesville just after sunrise. I had spent the night with Mother in order to look after Grandma Reynolds, who was very ill and had to have someone with her constantly. As I neared our house, I noticed a lot of cars, including some police cars, parked around the home of Mrs. Harris, an elderly neighbor who lived alone on her farm. When I got home, I asked Calvin, "What happened at Mrs. Harris' house?"

He didn't know, having just gotten out of bed. "I haven't heard anything about it," he said.

Around eight o'clock, after Calvin left for work, a car pulled into the driveway and Connie jumped out and ran up the walk. She seemed upset and distraught. I opened the door quickly to let her in. She sat down in the living room and began to fidget, ringing her handkerchief. There were deep circles under her eyes, and they were swollen and bloodshot. She'd been crying for quite a while. "Connie, whatever is the matter?" I exclaimed.

"Have you seen Jack?"

"No, I haven't. Why do you ask?"

Tearfully, she began telling me what had happened during the predawn hours of that day. Being in desperate need of money, she and Jack had planned to rob my neighbor, Mrs. Harris. "We heard she had a lot of money hidden in her house," Connie said. "So I let Jack out of the car just before sunrise, after we agreed to meet at your house in case of trouble. But when I went back to pick him up, I heard gun shots!" She looked at me with a silent plea for help and understanding.

I was stunned, and knew then that they only renewed their friendship with us for the purpose of using us, if they had to. They'd been planning this robbery for some time.

Connie continued, "Myrle, I tell you I don't know whether Jack shot Mrs. Harris, or she shot Jack! I just drove away without waiting to find out." She picked up

130

her purse and walked to the front door. "If you hear anything, will you telephone me?" And she left a number where she could be reached before running to her car, and screeching out the driveway.

As soon as she sped out of sight, I got in my car and drove past Mrs. Harris' farm. But I couldn't see what was happening. Then I went to the home of a neighbor to find out if they had heard anything. They told me that Mrs. Harris had been pistol-whipped and shot three times early that morning, as she stepped into the garage next to her house to get some feed for her chickens. Bleeding badly, she had picked up something from the floor of the garage and fought off her attacker. He ran, and she dragged herself to her car and drove to a nearby house for help. The police hadn't found her assailant, and had no clues as to his identity.

But I knew who it was.

I felt heartsick driving back home, and spent the rest of the morning praying and pacing the floor. I had been a Christian for only a few months, and before that I had always lived by the code of the streets: never "rat" on anyone. If you did, you got yours! Now I felt torn by conflicting loyalties. I thought of poor Mrs. Harris in the hospital, perhaps dead by now. (I'm thankful to say that, by the mercy of God, she recovered.) I thought about Jack, who had been through so much with Calvin and me and who had already served two terms in the penitentiary. I felt I could not be the one responsible for having him spend the rest of his life behind bars, like a caged animal.

By noon, I could stand it no longer, and I drove over to Pastor Shelton's house. It was hard for me to tell him about our involvement with Connie and Jack, because I was afraid he might think I had something to do with the crime. I hesitated for only a moment, however, because I knew that Jack might shoot someone else if he wasn't caught.

To my surprise, Paster Shelton didn't look at me with contempt, but was very understanding. He told me, "Christians should always do what is right, Myrle, regardless of the consequences." When I told him I feared for the safety of my family if I went to the police, he assured me, "If you do what is right and trust God, He will take care of you. I'm not going to tell you what to do," he added, "but I will pray with you and ask God to let you know the next step to take."

After we prayed, I drove to the police station and told everything to the officer in charge, including the fact that I was a friend of Jack's and that Jesus had given me a new life when I took Him as my Savior. After what He had done for me, I didn't want to go back on Him by not obeying God.

To my complete surprise, the policeman thanked me cordially and asked me to let him know if we heard any more from Jack or Connie. I knew I had obeyed God's will in going to the police station, and—in spite of my sadness for my old friends—I felt as though a great weight had been lifted from my shoulders. The police picked up Connie at her apartment, but they couldn't find Jack.

Around ten o'clock that night, there was a knock at our door and the dog began barking fiercely. When Calvin opened the door, Jack was standing there in the rain, soaked to the skin. He eyed us savagely. I knew instantly he was high on dope. "Calvin," he demanded, "take me to Middletown. I've got to see Connie." Calvin didn't argue with him—but as he and Jack went out to get into our car, he gave me a signal to show which way they were going. I called the police, who set up a roadblock and stopped the car. Jack was arrested and sent to jail to await trial.

Calvin and I dreaded appearing as witnesses against Jack at his hearing. But when the summons came the following December, we faced it together. It was indeed a trying experience, especially since Jack's attorney tried to prove that we were incompetent witnesses. He had a lot of garbage to draw from, too! Nevertheless, when I was on the witness stand, I gave my testimony of what Jesus had done for me and my family. Jack sat there with his head down as though in deep contemplation. I wondered if he was remembering what Connie had said on the way home from the Bible study. "I turned down the Lord," she'd said. "From now on it'll be real trouble."

Or, perhaps he was thinking about his Christian mother and the way she had taught him to love the Lord. After the sentence was passed, Jack thanked the judge for his time and ironically wished us all a Merry Christmas. Turning, handcuffed, he walked out of the courtroom with his eyes straight ahead. He never looked at Calvin and me.

We have heard by the grapevine that Connie is out of the women's prison now after spending five long years behind bars. We pray for both Jack and Connie that they might have another chance to find Jesus Christ and accept Him as their Savior. I've learned it is never too late for any of us. Look where I was when God found me! I was truly "in a desert land, in the howling void of the wilderness; He kept circling around [me], He

133

scanned [me] (penetratingly), He kept [me] as the pupil of His eye" (Deuteronomy 32:10 *AMP*).

Life has not always been easy since Calvin and I met the Lord—but when the trials come, we remember Paul's words to the early Christians in Rome: "If God is for us, who can be against us?" (Romans 8:31 *NIV*).

Chapter 21

From Death to Life

Grandma Reynolds, who was still living with Mother, was ninety-one years old when she went to be with Jesus, soon after Calvin commited his life to the Lord. She had been saved as a girl and had always said, "I love Jesus." My brother Gregg and his family came from their home in Wooster, Ohio, for the funeral. On the way to the mortuary, Gregg remarked about the wonderful change in Calvin and me. Of course we told him we'd been born again (John 3:3).

"I'm happy for you," Gregg said, "but I just can't go along with some of the words you use like 'born again,' 'saved,' and 'washed in the blood.' I've gone to church all my life and believe I've lived a good, moral life." He continued, "I'm satisfied with what I've got, even though an experience like your's and Calvin's might be necessary for some people."

The minister who conducted the funeral preached a sermon on salvation. He told us how much Grandma would love to have all of her loved ones with her in heaven some day. How I praise God for that preacher!

After the service at the cemetery, each of us

reminisced about Grandma and what she had meant to us. In the living room of Mother's house, Gregg began to talk to Calvin and me and, one by one, the others left the room. Calvin and I asked him, "Would you like to know for sure you will see Grandma again some day? Would you like to pray with us and ask Jesus to come into your heart?"

He said he would, and we were privileged to pray with Gregg as he repented of his sins and asked Christ to be his personal Savior. How happy Grandma must be knowing that Gregg had commited his life to the Lord on the day of her coronation in heaven!

The next day, before Gregg and his family started home, he came to our church for the Sunday morning service. As we sang the invitation hymn, Gregg walked forward to the altar with long strides and acknowledged Jesus publicly. Public confession is important because Jesus said in Matthew 10:32-33 (*NIV*), "Whoever acknowledges me before men, I will also acknowledge him before my Father in heaven. But whoever disowns me before men, I will disown him before my Father in heaven."

Not long after Gregg came to the Lord, my sister Jean found peace with God at a miracle service we attended in Pittsburgh. We had gone there to hear Kathryn Kuhlman and to see the Lord do His wonderful ministry of healing through her—and we weren't disappointed! As the Spirit of God began to move in that huge auditorium, the power was so strong I began to weep and tremble. While the congregation stood with their hands raised in praise to heaven, God began to heal people of every conceivable illness.

After the service, Miss Kuhlman gave the invitation

to all those who had not had a conversion experience to come and accept Jesus as Savior. My sister was one of the many who went forward to give herself to Christ.

I was so pleased that my brother Gregg had opened his heart's door to Jesus and delighted with Jean's conversion, but I think I was touched even more when some of my children decided to follow the Lord.

Each summer, a busload of young people from the Ridgeville church, along with several adults, made an overnight trip to Camp Maranatha in Muskegon, Michigan, for a week-long retreat. Most of the time was spent in the great outdoors, in fellowship with our Lord Jesus and with Christians from other local churches. Talent contests and sport contests of all kinds—shuffleboard, volleyball, horseshoes, softball, and track events—always made the week fly by. I have wonderful memories of swimming in the pool that overlooks Lake Michigan, walking through the green woods, and climbing up to the prayer tower, where I could look out over the lake and worship my Lord.

The summer of 1970 is especially memorable, because three of my sons—Kevin (then fourteen years old), and Gregg (twelve years old)—both of whom were living with my mother—and Calvin, Jr., (then eight years old) were in the group that went to camp. Calvin didn't go that year because he had to work. We left the church in Ridgeville at midnight on Sunday and arrived in camp late Monday morning. Camp officially opened with the evening meal in the dining hall.

After supper, everyone went over to the first worship service in the chapel, a rustic building open on three sides, with hewn logs for seats. A service was held there every evening and was followed by "family devotions"—the children meeting in small groups with their counselors, and the adults from our church meeting with Pastor Shelton. God spoke to our hearts very tenderly at those gatherings—and for me, this was the highlight of the day.

As the week went on, I began to doubt that my two older boys, Kevin and Gregg, were going to be saved. Still very young in the Lord, I hadn't learned how to trust Him the way He wants us to. By Wednesday night I was so burdened with concern for my boys that I decided to go to my room after chapel, instead of attending the devotional meeting. I got in bed and lay there crying and praying, pouring my heartache out to my heavenly Father. "Lord," I told Him, "I've been trying so hard, so very hard, to do everything the way You want me to do it. But nothing seems to be working out the way I had expected concerning my boys' salvation."

It seemed His peace settled upon me, and He said, *"Myrle, quit trying so hard and just trust Me. I know the desires of your heart, and I will grant them in My own time and in My own way."*

"Lord," I said, before drifting off to sleep, "I just don't know how You're going to work it all out." But somehow I felt confident He would.

The next morning, as I stood in the breakfast line in front of the dining hall, one of the children from our church came running up in great excitement to tell me, "Gregg was saved last night in devotions! Gregg has accepted Jesus as his Savior!" What joy flooded my whole being! My legs felt so weak I leaned against the building for support. As the sun rose higher on a new day, I prayed with thankfulness and relief, "Jesus,

You've done it again! And I thank You!"

At the Friday night service in the chapel, all who had taken Jesus as their Savior that week went forward to confess Him openly. Gregg was among those who went to kneel at the altar. To my added joy, Kevin was with him. And suddenly, I saw little Calvin standing there, too, with a counselor's arm around his shoulders. He had gone forward for a rededication of his life to Christ.

Actually, he was the first and the youngest in the family to invite Jesus into his heart. The summer before he had gone to camp and one of the preachers drove a stake into the ground and told him, "Every time you doubt your salvation and the commitment you've made this day, just remind Satan of this stake in the ground...a stake we placed here when you opened your heart and let Jesus make His home there." Calvin, Jr., never forgot that experience, and he has remained a faithful and steadfast follower of our Lord.

Chapter 22

God and the Housing Shortage

Calvin and I had been living a hand-to-mouth existence during most of our life together. Alcoholics and drug users seldom have enough money for the necessities of life—far less for any luxuries. Shortly after Calvin was born again, God began to show us that He works miracles in the economic, as well as in the spiritual and physical realms.

The Saturday after Calvin's salvation experience, we held an auction out on the farm where we had been living. The eight large rooms of that old farmhouse were furnished with antiques we'd collected and refinished. We sold everything, except the absolute necessities, and used the money to pay off every bill we owed, so we could make a fresh start in serving the Lord.

A short time later, Pastor Shelton passed out a book to every member of his congregation. It was entitled *Seed Faith* by Oral Roberts. We took it home, read it carefully, and decided to apply the seed-faith principle in our lives. Giving to God first out of our need—as you would put a seed in the ground, expecting it to grow and multiply—we then expected God to multiply it and meet our every need.

After we finished *Seed Faith*, we realized we *needed* to give. It was never convenient because we hardly had enough money for groceries. Out of our food money, we began holding back a few dollars each week to give to the Lord. We trusted Him to multiply it because it was taking all of our faith to give it. That was how we began to prosper.

Soon after we began applying the seed-faith principle, Calvin came home from work and asked, "How would you like to own the service station where I've worked for the past eight years?" His boss, although still a young man, had decided to retire and let Calvin have first chance at buying the dealership.

My human reaction was, "Calvin, where in the world could we get enough money to do this?" To purchase the dealership, Calvin would have to have at least $5,000. Money was tight, and it was very difficult to get a loan on anything at that time, especially for people with our credit rating. It *looked* humanly impossible. However, we have learned that *nothing* is impossible with God. We felt that He wanted us to have the dealership, and that if we were right, He would supply the money to buy it. We prayed earnestly about the situation, and as an act of faith Calvin filled out the dealership application and sent it into the oil company, leaving the space about financial resources blank. The application was accepted, and now all Calvin needed was $5,000! And he had ten days to raise it.

One morning, Calvin's boss told him all he'd heard so far was talk, and he wanted to see some cash that very day! Calvin assured him the Lord would provide; then he got into the car he was test driving after repairs, and drove around just talking to God. He told Him he had done all he could, and the rest was up to Him. The Lord would have to supply the money before the day was over. Then he went back to work and left the problem in God's hands.

Around three o'clock that afternoon, a friend of ours whom Calvin hadn't seen for months walked into the station, bringing his little girl's bicycle tire to have it patched. When he saw Dan, Calvin knew God had sent him, and that the miracle he'd been expecting was standing right there. Without wasting time on small talk, Calvin asked Dan, "Will you loan me $5,000?" Dan's reply was that he had half of that amount and his wife had the other half, but that they were getting a divorce, which would be final in three days. At Calvin's request, however, he agreed to go talk to his wife and call him back.

Within the hour, Dan called to say he and his wife had reconciled and had both agreed to lend Calvin the money. Before the day was over, they had been to the lawyer's office to have the necessary papers drawn up, and Calvin had the cash in hand to buy the dealership from his boss! Now the station belonged to our Father in heaven, with the Calvin Morris family as junior partners!

That same spring, Calvin outsold every other station under the same oil company's name. And in six months, he paid back the $5,000 he'd borrowed from Dan with ten percent interest. It was a miracle, because when Calvin opened for business the first day, he only had $20 to put in the cash register for change! To top it off, after the first year of such phenomenal success, the oil company sent representatives to Dayton to interview

143

Calvin. How we did laugh with joy when they asked, "Can you tell us how you did it?" We told them, of course, but they had difficulty understanding it. It just didn't fit into secular thinking.

God owns the cattle on a thousand hills (Psalm 50:10). Everything He possesses, He has given to Jesus Christ, and when we are His we become joint-heirs with Christ (Romans 8:17). Jesus says, "Give, and it will be given to you. A good measure, pressed down, shaken together and running over, will be poured into your lap. For with the meausre you use, it will be measured to you" (Luke 6:38 *NIV*). Giving proved to be the only way out of poverty for us. And we even found it to be the answer to our housing need, too.

After we auctioned off our furnishings for the farmhouse, we moved to Springboro, Ohio, a small town about three miles from Ridgeville. By this time, Kevin had come to live with us, and we were now a family of five—Calvin, me, Calvin, Jr., Tommy and Kevin. For one year we lived in a tiny three-room apartment over an old store building. It was such a dinky place, and we were so cramped there. The walls were of chipped white plaster. It had a miniature kitchen with an old sink, a small refrigerator, a compact stove and a rickety old table and chairs. There wasn't one room where I could lay a nine-foot-by-twelve-foot rug!

But it was the only apartment available in Springboro, and that's why we took it. You can believe we learned how to get along together that year! We had to—there wasn't any place to go for quiet thoughts or privacy! It was here we started our Christian lives and where the Lord blessed us in so many ways.

Near the end of our year there, my daughter, Lynn—who was now married and had a dear little boy, Scottie—moved into a new home with a fully equipped kitchen. She offered to sell us her almost new refrigerator-freezer and electric stove. Although we had no money saved and didn't even have room for these appliances in our apartment, I wanted them badly. That night in our prayers, we asked God to work a miracle if He wanted us to have them. As we prayed, the Lord impressed me to go to the bank and ask for the money, even though we had no collateral or credit references.

Before I went to the bank the next day, I asked Jesus to give me the right words to say to the loan officer. When I got there, I marched up to his desk, looked him straight in the eyes, and told him boldly, "I need $200 to buy a refrigerator and stove at a real bargain." Without asking any questions, he took out the proper form, filled it out for me, and handed it to me for Calvin and me to sign. When I took it back to him the next day with our signatures in the designated place, he looked it over before counting out $200 and handing it to me. Just like that! Only a year and a half earlier, we couldn't have borrowed as much as one dollar if our lives had depended on it. Jesus made the difference!

Two days after that incident, a Christian friend of mine told me one of her neighbors was moving away and had a washer and a dryer to sell. She was asking just $25.00 for each of them. After inspecting the machines, I couldn't believe the price, for they were in perfect conditon. Never before had I owned an automatic washer or a dryer! We stored our four new appliances with some friends, and seven days later I bought a pretty damask sofa from a member of our congregation. That very afternoon a real estate agent came to our small apartment and asked, "How would you people like to move?"

I chuckled. "Are you kidding? We sure would, but there are no places to rent here in Springboro."

She smiled. "I've found you a nice, unfurnished apartment that has just been vacated. It has lots of room—three bedrooms, a bath, and a living room dining room combination. I could have rented it to a lot of people, but a close friend of mine who goes to your church had asked me try to locate a place for you. As a favor to her, I'm giving you first chance at this apartment."

The rent was reasonable, and the apartment was everything we had hoped for. We still had our beds from the farmhouse, so all we had to do was pick up the refrigerator, stove, washer, dryer and couch, and move in. God had provided for us! The Bible says He will supply all our need "according to his glorious riches in Christ Jesus" (Philippians 4:19 *NIV*).

Our new apartment was located across the street from the high school, and we took advantage of its location to tell the kids about Jesus. Each week we hung in our front window—which was right on the street—a picture of Christ or a poster about salvation, trying to select the kind that appeals to teenagers. We also put in the window each week a different scripture verse printed with large letters on a little card. The window was illuminated by a light that burned twenty-four hours a day.

We had a lot of response to our "advertisements." Some kids would come in to talk and ask questions.

146

Others never missed reading the Bible verse every week.

We also sponsored several parties for the teenagers. And once, when a musical group known as "The Living Sound" sang at the Ridgeville church, we invited them after the service to a party in our apartment. Just before the party ended, we noticed two young hitchhikers sitting on our front step listening to the fun going on inside. We invited them in, and Christian kids witnessed to them for a couple of hours.

We had been living in this larger apartment for about a year when my Avon lady stopped in to tell me she was also selling real estate. "I know a place that's just right for you and your family," she said. It was a three-bedroom, ranch-type house, set under many shade trees on two acres of land, with plenty of room for a big garden. Perhaps the feature that appealed to us most was a swimming pool in the back yard. The boys and I went delirious over the house immediately, but Calvin was more cautious. Only after much prayer and consideration did we finally buy it.

The Lord had prospered us beyond my dreams. Through a nationwide gas station contest which Calvin won, the Lord even threw in a belated honeymoon trip to Hawaii! My cup of happiness was bubbling over! As Calvin and I stood looking out over the wide expanse of the Pacific Ocean from high up on our hotel balcony, we felt a surge of gratitude that knew no bounds. How precious this time was to us! We knew God had planned it all, just to show us His loving interest in our well being. He had given us a beautiful house, a successful business, and a honeymoon trip to Hawaii. How good He is!

Chapter 23

Twenty-Twenty Vision

One day, while I was meditating on scriptures related to the cross, I asked God to give me some light on the matter of divine healing. I couldn't understand why some people were healed and others weren't. I knew that God is no respecter of persons—so if He would heal one, why wouldn't He heal another? All of a sudden, the answer came to me: God's promises are for every person, but not every one has claimed them by believing them.

I believe that one of the greatest biblical truths is found in Isaiah 53:4-5 (*AMP*): "Surely He (Jesus) has borne our griefs—sickness, weakness and distress—and carried our sorrows and pain [of punishment]. Yet we ignorantly considered Him stricken, smitten and afflicted by God [as if with leprosy]. But He was wounded for our transgressions, He was bruised for our guilt and iniquities; the chastisement needful to obtain peace and well-being for us was upon Him, and with the stripes that wounded Him we are healed and made whole."

Not only did Christ bare our sins on the cross; He also bore our sicknesses. God does not want His children to sin, nor does He want them to be sick.

God sent His Son to die on the cross for my sins two thousand years ago so that I no longer have to be a sinner. He bore all my sin on the cross so that all I have to do is accept my salvation by faith. Now the Bible says in Hebrews 11:1 (*NIV*) that "faith is being sure of what we hope for and certain of what we do not see."

I didn't *look* saved the day I took Jesus as my Savior, and I didn't particularly *feel* saved every day after that. But I *was* saved. Why? Because God's Word said I was, and I believed it. All right then: Jesus also carried my sicknesses, so all I have to do is accept Him as my Healer—again, by faith.

When I grasped this truth, it put a new sparkle in my life. If Jesus suffered so much so I could have healing and forgiveness of sins, I should certainly accept these gifts. He also became poor, so that I could have riches. Paul says in 2 Corinthians 8:9 (*NIV*), "For you know the grace of our Lord Jesus Christ, that though he was rich, yet for your sakes he became poor, so that you through his poverty might become rich." He has done it *all*!

The Bible doesn't say I won't sin any more; but when I do make a mistake, I have an advocate in my precious Lord Jesus, who pleads my case to the Father. If I confess my sins, God is faithful to forgive me of my sins (1 John 1:9). God has also provided for my healing. Members of our family still get sick, but all we have to do when we recognize the symptoms is to say, "Satan, you can stop trying to make God out a liar. The Word says I was healed two thousand years ago, by Jesus' stripes. I believe I'm saved, and I believe I'm healed! These symptoms you are trying to put on me will have to go—because I refuse to believe anything other than the very Word of God. I don't go by my feelings or by what I sense, see, or smell. I walk by faith, and I refuse to accept these symptoms in the name of the Lord Jesus Christ of Nazareth!"

The Bible also tells us, in the gospel of Mark 6:13 (*NIV*), what Jesus' disciples did for the sick: "They ... anointed many sick people with oil and healed them." And we know that as Jesus' disciples today, we have the same power as the disciples did then, if we will only have the faith.

We in the Morris family haven't always succeeded in following God's directions on healing, and as a result we have failed Him many times; but God has never failed us. Whenever we *believed* Him for our healing, He has always met our need. When the children are sick, Calvin asks them if they want to believe God for their healing. If they do, we anoint them with oil and pray for them, and they are healed. God never fails; He is not in the failing business.

Sometimes the children don't want to pray but would rather go to the doctor. In that case, we take them. Praise God for doctors! But there is a better way, and as the children have grown in faith and maturity, we have proved it more and more. It always works if we only believe without wavering between two opinions (James 1:6-8). The choice is ours. God has provided healing for us.

Soon after my study in this subject, I had been reading for several hours when I began having some very sharp pain in and behind my eyes. In just a few minutes, I was almost blind! The light hurt my eyes so badly I had to keep them closed. I panicked! Tommy and Gregg happened to be home at the time, and they rushed me to the clinic in Springboro. The doctor said I was hemorrhaging behind my eye balls and gave me an injection to ease the pain. He called an eye specialist immediately.

Only after the drug took effect and the pain was gone did I remember to pray. Sounds awful, doesn't it? How could I forget to pray? Well, I learned something that day. We are so used to accepting what our physical senses tell us that we automatically believe what we feel. I found it can be difficult, but not impossible, to walk by faith in the face of severe pain or illness.

As I lay there on a table waiting for the specialist, I heard the Holy Spirit whispering, way down inside of me: *"By His stripes you are healed! Jesus bore this on the cross; you don't have to have it!"* Over and over again those words were repeated. The drug affected my mind and body, but it couldn't touch my spirit, and down in my spirit the Holy Spirit had gotten through to me.

When the specialist came, I knew I was fine. And when he examined me, he couldn't find anything wrong with my eyes. He became very angry and accused me of faking my symptoms just to get a shot. He knew my past history, and didn't believe me when I told him that Jesus freed me from my addiction when I met Him at the foot of the cross and starting living for Him.

As he went out the door, he muttered, "There's nothing the matter with either of your eyes. You have twenty-twenty vision!"

I praised God for healing me again, and asked His forgiveness for the times of doubt and unbelief, and the times I have failed to receive all He has provided for me through His beloved Son.

Chapter 24

An Old Enemy

When I lived in Ridgeville as a teenager, the church had no pastor and only about twenty-seven members. Students from a seminary in Dayton took turns coming out to preach on Sundays. Today, there is a new church building, a parsonage, and lots of land for future expansion. Recently, the church opened a Christian school which includes a kindergarten and classes for first through eighth grades.

In September, 1972, the church conducted a week-long revival led by Dr. Eric Hutchings, an international radio evangelist. There was a great flow of the Holy Spirit among the people every night. Souls were saved, and many Christians received more of God.

Dr. Hutchings' broadcast is heard around the world and even in Russia. It is beamed from gospel radio station Trans World Radio from Monaco, a tiny Mediterranean principality. While he conducted meetings in our church, Dr. Hutchings tape recorded an interview with Pastor Shelton for his program and then Calvin and I had the thrill of telling what Christ had done for us. It was taped in our home and broadcast during his radio program in the fall of 1973. Millions heard our testimony, and we prayed that many were won to the Kingdom of God because of it.

About a month after Dr. Hutchings' visit, the Lord brought to my mind the face of an old enemy, Ellen. A few years earlier, before I came to know the Lord, a trip to a familiar Middletown bar had been almost my last time to go anywhere.

One evening when I went out to drink, some of the gang thought it would be amusing to see me and my girlfriend, Ellen, fight. Ellen was about six feet tall and notorious for the fights she'd had and the people she'd whipped. I felt safe running around with her, especially when I ran out of money. She protected me from the others when they didn't want me around any longer.

Ellen didn't "pop" pills. She was crazy enough on hard liquor. Sometimes she took a diet pill with her whiskey, but she didn't take drugs as much as I did. That night the gang waited until she and I were drinking. We took some diet pills and were feeling a little high. Then they told her, "Hey, Ellen! Myrle's been out with your man!"

It was true I had taken him in my car to visit some of his relatives one night when he was looking for her. But I had not been with him under any other circumstances. It was a vulgar lie, but in her condition, she believed them. I never had a chance to defend myself. Ellen went beserk. Before I could blink an eyelid she'd thrown me to the floor, grabbed a steel barstool and was using it to beat me over the head. She had all the strength of a female grizzly. One leg of the stool cut my left eyebrow wide open to the bone, and blood spurted everywhere. My hair was soon matted with blood, and my arms became bruised and battered as I tried to ward off her blows. When I could hold my arms up no longer, I tried to crawl away from her. She pulled out a six-inch knife and stabbed me in the hip. I rolled over onto my back just in time to see the knife blade coming down again—this time toward my stomach. Somewhere, from the depth of my being, a name formed, took shape and exploded. I cried out, "Jesus!" with such power and authority she stopped dead still. She stood up, confused. She handed the knife to a man who was watching and ran out of the tavern and into the night.

When I finally got to my feet—no one cared enough to help me—I drank two double shots of vodka straight down, staggered to a phone, and called Calvin. The bartender was mopping my blood off the floor when he arrived. As soon as he stepped in the door and saw me, he said, "I'm taking you to the hospital!"

"No," I said in a hard, flat voice. "Take me home!" And I refused to be treated. When I got home I passed out on the bed and laid there for almost two hours. When the drinks and pills wore off, I got up and looked in the mirror. Seeing my face almost sent me into shock! "I'm a creature from hell!"

There was a very deep gash over my left eye, and the skin was laid back, revealing the bone. There was dried blood all over my face and clothes. My hair was disheveled and matted with blood. From the stab wound in my hip, I had blood all over my jeans. There were black and blue marks all over me. "Calvin!" I screamed uncontrollably. "Take me to the hospital!"

The cut over my eye left a scar that will never go away. Every time I look in the mirror, I am reminded of that awful night and those years of living in hell on this earth.

But now, just a few years later, the Lord was continually bringing Ellen's face to my mind. Finally, one day as I was fixing lunch I reached over to the phone and dialed her number. When she answered the phone, I could tell she'd been crying. She told me she was very ill with diabetes. As we talked, she kept repeating, "I'm not taking my insulin today because I want to die."

"Ellen," I said, "if you go to the hospital, I promise to come and see you every day while you're there." I kept that promise, and other people from our church also visited her.

After Ellen got out of the hospital, she and Larry, her husband, began coming to our church occasionally. One month, they were there every night for a week of basic Bible teaching. The final meeting of the series was on Friday night, and a praise service followed. As we began to sing and worship God, a message was given in tongues and then interpreted (1 Corinthians 14:5). We raised our hands in thanksgiving to our heavenly Father, and as we gave our voices over to the Holy Spirit, we began to sing. As we continued, the melody of worship and praise took on a quality of unearthly beauty.

Then the power of God fell on the congregation, and Ellen began to sob aloud. Some of the church people came over and laid hands on her head. Their prayers broke the chains of the enemy that had bound her all her life, and she lifted her voice to God, "Forgive me, forgive me!" Unable to get beyond that point, she explained to those ministering to her, "I don't know how to pray." The Christians surrounding her, gently lifted her arms in the name of Jesus Christ. Immediately, she had freedom to praise Jesus and thanked Him for what He had done for her.

I was crying like a baby as we worshipped together before the King of Glory. Here we were—sisters in crime who had almost destroyed each other only a few years ago—now sisters in Christ, loving each other with God's divine love.

Chapter 25

The Big Move

Shortly after we moved to our beautiful new home with the swimming pool, the Lord began to open the doors to a ministry we had never anticipated. Through a dear little sister in Christ, we met a young man, Blaine Bowman, who had given his heart to the Lord that year at a Full Gospel Business Men's Fellowship International Convention. His vitality and enthusiasm for Jesus endeared him to our hearts immediately.

One night when Blaine was swimming in our pool, he shared his desire to minister to young people. Blaine really felt the Lord was calling him into a full-time ministry. As he looked around our spacious grounds he commented, "What a beautiful place to have a Jesus Rally!" Although a little surprised, Calvin and I prayed about it and received a clear message from the Lord to open our home to these kids, not just for a one-time rally, but for weekly meetings.

Every Friday night throughout that summer, we had over one hundred teenagers at our home, receiving the love of Jesus. Blaine and his talented sister, Diane, had formed a singing group called "The Children of Light."

They provided the music for the young people's meetings and Blaine did all the preaching and sharing of God's Word. Our son, Tom, even played drums with them for a while before he had to return to college.

It was such a fruitful and exciting ministry. Just hearing those young voices raised to Jesus often brought tears to my eyes. Calvin felt the same way. It made us remember how lost and rebellious we both were as young people. And it made us glad to have in our home teenagers from all over the county joining together to celebrate their love for Jesus. It was too bad that one of the teenagers in my own house wasn't a part of those weekly gatherings. My son, Kevin, wasn't joining in like he used to. He was becoming strangely restless, and I atttributed his behavior to a passing stage. "He'll be okay," I told myself. So I wasn't overly concerned about him at the time.

I was so happy in Ridgeville that leaving was one of the farthest things from my mind. But the Lord had other plans. Calvin and I took a trip to Morris Fork, Kentucky, to visit his relatives and were surprised to find that Grandpa Morris wanted to sell the old home-place where Calvin was raised. When Calvin thought of that beautiful piece of land (over 300 acres), with the tree-covered mountains and rich, green valleys, he couldn't bear to let it go. It was Calvin's long time dream to live in Morris Fork, the haunt of his childhood. And of course, loving the outdoors the way I do, I knew I could be happy there, too. After we prayed about it, Calvin had all the legal papers drawn up and paid Grandpa for the property. It was ours now, but should it be our permanent home?

As Calvin and I continued to seek the Lord's

direction, Jesus reminded us of the gasoline shortage that was causing Calvin's profits in the service station to decline with each passing week. It was 1974 and none of the gas stations could get enough gas to supply their customers. Also, Calvin had received an offer months before to become the service manager for a car dealership in Jackson, Kentucky, just twenty-six miles from the Morris Fork homestead. At the time, we hadn't even considered it. But now we could see the Lord providing another open door for the move to Kentucky.

Because Calvin and I wanted to be sure of God's will, we felt led to take one final step. We put our house up for sale and asked a much higher price than we had paid for it just a few months before. Calvin prayed earnestly, "Lord, if You really want this family to move back to Kentucky, please let someone buy the house for this price." We even set a deadline for the sale of the house, or else we were staying in Ohio.

Would you believe it? It dragged on, right up to the last day, and then the Lord miraculously provided a buyer. The whole matter was settled in just a matter of days and we were on our way to Calvin's childhood playground in the Cumberland Mountains.

I knew I would dearly miss Ridgeville and the friends who ministered to me the five years I'd walked among them. I was sad when we left, leaving our beautiful home with the swimming pool. Although I knew there would be new friends waiting for us in the mountains of Kentucky, it was difficult to let go of those who'd taught me so much in those first years when I was learning about the Lord.

But what a beautiful, rustic setting we live in now! A creek in the front yard, and a waterfall by the barn! No swimming pool, but a swimming hole. No cars whizzing by our home; just peace and quiet, the sound of gentle breezes rustling the branches and leaves of tall trees.

We have no telephone, and we waited almost a year before hooking up a television set. We have many friendly neighbors who live along the creek, and we belong to the little Morris Fork mission church founded by Uncle Sammie. At church, we sit on handmade chairs with handwoven hickory bark seats. The young missionary pastor who was here until recently, Allen McCrane, with his young wife, Linda, had their hands full ministering in two different churches—one of which was Morris Fork.

Calvin, Jr., now a tall, broad-shouldered sixteen-year-old, loves to hunt and fish and work the farm. He rides twenty-six miles on a school bus to Jackson, Kentucky, to school. My training from long ago comes in handy now. Remember when those ladies in Quicksand taught me how to can? It was a good thing I learned, because I can a lot of vegetables in the summertime.

Something wonderful happened soon after we moved to Morris Fork. It was in February, and Calvin, Calvin, Jr., and I were up in the corn field on our farm, picking some fresh corn for dinner. Calvin's brother, Dale, his wife, Judy, and her sister, Evelyn, came walking into the hollow. Dale was on his crutches—he'd lost a leg in a bulldozer accident a couple of years earlier. They had just recently received Christ as Savior and were waiting for a nice day so they could be baptized in the creek. "Can you go with us?" Dale asked. "Let's see if we can find the preacher and get him

162

to baptize Judy and me."

We all agreed it was a perfect day to follow the Lord in water baptism, so dressed as we were, we went to the church to find Pastor Allen. "I'll be glad to baptize you and Judy," he told Dale. Then turning to Calvin, he added, "Calvin, think you can round up one of the elders and a deacon?"

"Sure can, Pastor," Calvin said. We all arrived at the waterhole around five o'clock. Some curious onlookers in cars and pickup trucks stopped by the side of the road to witness the baptism. We sang some songs and praised the Lord. When it was time to enter the icy water, Calvin, overalls and all, went and helped Pastor Allen baptize Dale and Judy. It was a special treat for him to participate in his own brother's baptism.

Later that evening, we went to Dale and Judy's for supper. We put our steaks on the stove and sat around talking about the goodness of God when a knock came on the door. It was Pastor Allen and his sweet wife, Linda. "The Lord sent us," they said. "We want to talk to Dale and Judy about the baptism in the Holy Spirit."

We turned the stove off while Pastor Allen read a few scriptures showing Dale and Judy the reason why they needed the baptism of the Spirit. Just before he asked them if they were ready to receive more of Jesus, he turned to Calvin and asked, "Calvin, have you ever received the baptism in the Holy Spirit?"

"Well, I have prayed and asked the Holy Spirit to come in and control my life," Calvin responded. "But I have never spoken in tongues." He was quiet for a moment before going on, choosing his words carefully. "I've been kind of afraid of this experience. But with the Lord's help I've overcome that fear, and Preacher, with your help, I'm ready to receive if you'll pray with me."

Pastor Allen got three chairs from the kitchen and put them in the center of the very small living room with its linoleum floor and coal heating stove in the corner. There was such a sweet presence of the Holy Spirit in that room as we laid hands on Calvin, Dale and Judy. Calvin, Jr., had already received the Holy Spirit and spoken in tongues so he prayed with us for his Daddy. It was a glorious occasion. Calvin's face was upturned, his hands in the air reaching toward heaven, worshiping the Lord.

Evelyn, Judy's lovely teenage sister, was a silent witness to all the proceedings of that day. She is a beautiful mountain girl with long, flowing blond hair. After we prayed for the others, Pastor Allen asked her, "Evelyn, would you like to receive Christ as your Savior?"

"Yes, I'd love to," was her quiet answer. So Pastor Allen led her to the Lord while we all praised and sang in the Spirit. When we got home that night, Calvin, Jr., went right to sleep but Calvin and I couldn't sleep. We rolled and tossed until Calvin said, "Why don't we quit trying to sleep?" He got up and put on his bathrobe. "Let's pray."

I agreed and got out of bed, too. All we wanted to do was worship the Lord, so we followed our inclination and knelt by the side of our bed to praise Him. I don't know if Calvin later drifted off to sleep or not, but I know when I would fall asleep from time to time, my spirit continued to raise its hallelujahs to Jesus. I wasn't saying anything audibly, but I would wake up with a start and be worshiping the Lord from deep down inside my being.

The next morning, I got up refreshed and we went to church where Dale and Judy became official members of the little Morris Fork church. And Dale said to us that day, "Since Christ has come into our lives, everything seems to be 'going' for us. It just seems like everything is beginning to work out!"

Chapter 26

Trial by Fire

Today as I sit here and try to write the concluding chapters of this book, I have to agree with my brother-in-law, Dale. Yes, when Christ comes into our hearts everything is "going" for us, and the Lord can make all things work together for good if we love him (Romans 8:28). Knowing that and living it, however, was a difficult learning process for me.

I am discovering that this Christian walk is more than I had anticipated. I thought that after finding Jesus and getting baptized with the Spirit, my troubles were all over. I thought the Christian life was one big rainbow and I was really flying high most of the time. I was active in the church and ministered to others at every opportunity. I attended many conventions and retreats, heard a lot of speakers and bought many cassette tapes on spiritual themes to take home and study. "I'm growing in the Lord," I'd think, "and things couldn't be better."

Of course, I *was* growing in the Lord, and I did truly love Him. But a lot of the spiritual motions I was going through were only covering up some of the garbage lurking under the surface of my life. God wanted to deal with it, and I wanted to gloss it over. Things like unforgiveness, resentment and hostilities out of the past. There were a lot of things, I was soon to discover, that I hadn't really surrendered completely to the Lord.

How busy I was trying to *do* things for the Lord; and He, all the time, wanted me to *be* more like Him. Doing would be a natural outgrowth of being; I learned that later on. . . . And how I learned was, as usual, the hard way. You would think that after all I'd been through up to this point I'd stay close to the Savior. But I made a few compromises down the line and the results proved disastrous.

I would like to have ended this book leaving you with the impression of my great victorious walk with Jesus. It would have been so comfortable for you and for me, too. And everything would have been tied in such a neat bow. But the testimony of God's love and forgiveness toward me is so awesome that I must share the whole story. There is victory in the end, but it was not my victory. *It was the Lord's.*

For a while, anyway, everything seemed to be so wonderful, so perfect . . . until one evening, just a few months before our move to Kentucky. My seventeen-year-old son, Kevin, didn't come home from work. He was normally so punctual; you could set your clock by him. He was in his senior year of high school and worked for Calvin at the service station in the evenings. He would close up the station and bring the money home to Calvin. He didn't show up until three in the morning. We heard him coming in, and we called him into our bedroom. "Where have you been, Kevin?" I asked, annoyed at his late hour appearance. "We were concerned about you!"

"I was driving home," he began, "when I noticed a guy in another car following me. So I pulled over and he did too. He asked me for the directions to a neighbor's house. We talked for a while...."

Calvin lost his temper. "Now, look here, Kevin," he said heatedly, "I can't have you doing things like this with all that money on you. Don't you know you could have been mugged and robbed? If I can't depend on you to come straight home with the money, I'm not going to be able to let you stay and lock up for me."

Usually Kevin was very mannerly and would have apologized, but he just stood there and kept staring at us with a silly grin on his face. I couldn't see him distinctly because only the hall light was on, but as I looked at him, I got a sick feeling in the pit of my stomach. I sat up and turned on my reading lamp. "Come over here, Kevin, and let me look at you." He quietly came over to my side of the bed. I saw the pupils of his eyes were dilated and I recognized the symptoms of drugs.

"Calvin," I said with a heavy sigh, "there's no use talking to him now. He's high on some kind of drug." And I felt like the foundations of my secure little world were crumbling. "Go to bed, Kevin," I ordered with a firm voice, and when he left the room, I burst into tears.

Well, it was just the beginning of heartbreak like I've never known—because our precious boy, Kevin, took the path of drugs and turned his back on Christ and on his family. From that night on it was one phone call after another from different police stations.

So many times I would remember how tender he had been to the things of God, how touched he was, for instance, when a high school friend died. Kevin wept.

"Mom, I just can't quit thinking about this kid. Here he was alive one moment and gone the next, into eternity forever. Never to hear another record played, never to see his girlfriend again, never to see another sunrise and maybe to spend eternity in the lake of fire."

Even Calvin, who was listening, could see how upset Kevin was.

"Did you ever tell the boy about Jesus?" I asked.

"No," Kevin admitted. "That's the worst part of it."

Then Calvin entered into the conversation. "Sometimes," he explained, "God has a way of using bad things that have happened to open our eyes to how short our lives here on this earth really are. Like a blade of grass that soon withers and dies."

The three of us knelt and prayed, as Calvin thanked God for all He had done for us, and for showing us that we are only here, living and breathing, by the wonderful mercy and grace of our heavenly Father.

A few days after the boy's funeral, Kevin told me, "Mom, I want you to know that I've gotten my life straightened out with God." Again, big tears welled up in his eyes and splashed down his cheeks as he began telling me how God had shown him how precious life really is, and how he needed to have Christ in his heart. "I have been living a double life, Mom," he confessed. "I have tried to make you and Calvin believe I'm okay spiritually when all the time I really haven't been living for the Lord. But I'm going to walk with Him from now on."

Even now there are times when those words echo in my ears at night. If only it had been so. But that was Kevin before drugs. Because of what he put us through for some three years, I began to understand how my parents had suffered because of me. It has been twenty-nine years since I ran away from home the first time. Only now do I realize the torture I put my folks through. I can imagine how they sat, staring out the window, wondering where I was and if I was safe, or if I had enough to eat. They wondered if they would ever see me again. Their eyes were often swollen from crying all night long, waiting to receive news from me. Sometimes they sat up all night in the living room, waiting for the phone to ring, waiting to hear that I was all right. I've done the same thing myself, over and over again.

The first time Kevin ran away from home, we'd had an argument about marijuana. Calvin and I were shocked and hurt when we found out he and his friends had been smoking "grass" for several weeks.

Kevin and I hotly disagreed on the dangers of using this drug. I explained to him that young users often find their education interrupted and their future shadowed or altered because of a police record. I realize that marijuana is not a narcotic and does not cause physical dependence as heroin or other narcotics. But it can produce harmful side effects. It is dangerous to drive while under the influence of "grass." And it can mess up the user's personality, growth and development. When teenagers are having enough problems adjusting to adulthood, using drugs only causes more problems. Not to mention the Satanic, demonic forces that enter when a Christian turns his back on the Lord and allows himself to be pulled under the influence of the numerous drugs sweeping the country today. Sooner or later, someone in the group where the user is taking drugs, will "chicken" him into trying something stronger.

These were the arguments I offered Kevin, but he was past listening. And in his anger, he took off out the door. I made my way down the hall and into his bedroom. He was such a neat boy; his dresser drawers were always well-organized. Not like the other boys who were so messy. I had to continually remind them to hang up their clothes and not leave them kicking around the floor. But not Kevin; he was different.

He was shy and withdrawn; not as outgoing as the others. His manners were impeccable, and until he started using drugs, he was a top student in school. My heart was so burdened that day when he ran away for the first time. I prayed, "Lord, take care of Kevin. He's going in the wrong direction. You help him, Lord, and turn him around before it's too late."

Many years ago, my Daddy sat talking with me as tears coursed down his face. He told me, "Myrle, some day when you have teenagers you'll find out how much you've hurt Mother and me by being so rebellious." He said, "What you sow, you reap." He told me that someday I'd find out how it hurt to sit and worry and cry and wait for news of my children.

Well, it happened. I have sat here by my window, waiting, praying and trusting God to bring Kevin back home safely. I've gone to his room again and again and stood in the middle of the floor, weeping and praying over him. And remembering. . . . He was so happy in school, so proud of his grades. What happened? What went wrong? Why, oh why? I'd ask myself. He had given his life to Christ and seemed happy serving the Lord. Then, suddenly, everything changed.

The first thing Calvin and I noticed was Kevin's

disinterest in church. Then his studies began to slide. His mode of dress changed. He gave all his nice sport clothes away and began wearing worn-out blue jeans everywhere he went.

So many nights, Kevin would wander home, cold and hungry. Other evenings, we'd receive a phone call from the police in a nearby city. They wanted us to come and get our son. One officer called us at four in the morning and said, "We've got your son down here. He seems confused and frightened." When he got home, he told us he'd taken LSD and had experienced a very "bad" trip.

Now and then, a ray of hope would trickle through the blackness. Like the few times Kevin came into our bedroom in the wee hours of the night, asking us to pray with him. We were eager to do so. But more times, he'd go all to pieces when we tried to counsel him, getting hysterical over the tiniest matters.

On his high school graduation day, Kevin lacked two hours of getting all of his credits. They let him go through the motions of graduating with his friends, but he didn't get a diploma. He left home the next day.

About a month later, just after our move to the Morris Fork homestead, Kevin had a bad reaction to some drugs and my mother had to rush him to the hospital where they kept him for about a week. The hospital recommended a psychiatrist, but he only put Kevin on more drugs.

At Christmas, we got word through a friend of his that Kevin had been arrested for possession of drugs in the state of New Jersey. He had spent the holidays behind bars. He was beaten savagely by another inmate, and finally, after his trial, he was told, "Go home and never return to this state again.'' Kevin went back to my mother's house in Ohio and continued to use drugs every day. We prayed night and day for his deliverance.

The following Christmas he was in jail somewhere else. And the third year he was in jail in Lebanon, Ohio, which is close to where we used to live. I went to see him as often as I could. Shortly after, he was sent to the state penitentiary in Ohio, and a little bit of me went with him. It was just about more than I could bear. He got mixed up with kids who were breaking into peoples' homes and was sent up for armed robbery.

I blamed myself for Kevin's waywardness. I felt that if I had been the mother I should have been to him when he was growing up, perhaps this never would have happened. Memories would come back to me late at night. Memories of Kevin curled up in bed with a pair of my old pajamas for security. He needed me when he was little, and I'd been so selfishly involved with my own problems. And the more I dwelt on the past, the harder it became to trust the Lord.

I went to visit Kevin in prison. When those steel bars clanged open, he walked into the visiting room in his prison uniform, tall and handsome. I couldn't talk to him without crying. He was my baby, and I loved him.

He tried to console me. "Mom," he told me, "I've gotten right with God again. Jesus means everything to me." And he told me how the Lord had protected him from the homosexuals who tried to molest him. After several weeks in the penitentiary, Kevin was transferred to a correctional institute near Lebanon.

Then, in December, just before Christmas, Kevin was paroled and came back to live with us in Kentucky. I was elated! All I could do was laugh and cry. Mother and I went to pick him up, and when they opened those prison gates and Kevin walked through them, I could have danced before the Lord—like David of the Old Testament—and not been ashamed for all the prison administrators to see me. It was a joyous day, and I vowed silently, "He'll never go back to prison. I won't lose him again."

Chapter 27

The Crushing Weight

Kevin looked so good when he got out of prison. He'd kicked the drug habit during his six months of incarceration. And he was happy and chatty on our drive back to Mother's house in Waynesville where we planned to spend the night before leaving early the next morning for Morris Fork.

Mother prepared a delicious dinner for us and after some small talk, we all went to bed, exhausted over the events of the day. But I couldn't sleep. About two in the morning, I got out of bed and walked over to the window. It had begun to snow lightly. As I stood there, watching the snow fall, I saw Kevin underneath the light that burns all night in the barnyard. He was pacing back and forth like a trapped animal. I felt uneasy. I dressed as quickly as possible and went outside to where he was standing.

"Kevin, is there something wrong?"

"No," he said, slowly. "I just can't sleep. I think I'll take a walk and go downtown for a while." He looked at me wordlessly, and I felt that deep within him a fierce battle raged.

"If you want," I rushed on, "we can leave right now. We'll just go ahead to the mountains."

"No, Mom," he said, taking my arm and leading me back to the house. "I'll go to bed." He smiled, and I felt somewhat eased. We left Ohio early the next morning.

It was so wonderful to have Kevin home again in Kentucky. His first day there, the two of us hiked through the beautiful timber land and up through the hills and to the top of the ridge overlooking our house. It was crisp and cold as we sat and looked through his binoculars, enjoying the spectacular beauty of the snow-covered woods in winter. "Mom," he said, "it's so good to be home. I never, never want to go back to prison. It was such a horrible place."

"Kevin," I vowed, "I'll never let you go back."

A week later, I took him to Jackson where he took a test to get his high school diploma. He passed. Then we went to the enrollment office at Lee's college in Jackson and enrolled him for the following semester which started in early January.

"With Calvin working in Jackson," I told Kevin, "it'll be so convenient for you to go to college there. You can commute with Calvin every day."

A few days after Christmas, I had to drive Kevin back to Ohio to appear as a witness against the boys he had gotten in trouble with. We stayed in a motel because, as the police explained, "Your lives might be in danger if you stay with friends or relatives."

I felt keyed up and taunt. I'd been through so much worry and heartache for three years with Kevin. It never let up. I thought I had given my burden to the Lord to carry, but I hadn't really, because the full weight of it was on my shoulders. And it didn't belong there. I couldn't bear it. Oh, I wish I had just leaned upon Him and let Him support that crushing weight! But I didn't.

At supper that evening, I ordered Kevin a beer because he wanted one. "He's been in prison six months, and we're together for the first time in a long time," I rationalized. "He wants to have a good time, and I'm not going to be as strict as I've been before." I was compromising with Satan all the way. And to make matters worse, I even went a step further: would you believe I ordered several beers for myself and drank them? Me, an ex-alcoholic, marvelously delivered of alcoholism! Here I was—compromising on a major issue. But I was trying desperately to make up to Kevin for all he had gone through. Trying in my own feeble strength.

I knew Holy Spirit conviction that night! I didn't sleep. And I fell into Satan's trap: I felt so guilty that I couldn't pray. I felt I'd climbed back into a dark abyss. How was I to get out? I know now I should have fallen to my knees, confessed my sin, and been cleansed. But I didn't do that.

The next morning, Sunday, I was deathly sick. If I had been on a drunk for a month, I couldn't have been sicker. I thought I was going to die. Instead of going to church, Kevin took me to my daughter Lynn's house— against the advice of the detectives—and she fixed us something to eat. Her boyfriend—Lynn was divorced by then—lit up a marijuana cigarette and offered it to Kevin. "Do you want one?" he asked.

"Yes," Kevin said. And he smoked "pot" right in front of me. I began to cry.

"Don't cry, Mom," Lynn comforted. "He'll be all right in a couple of hours."

The next day I took Kevin to the hearing and that afternoon we returned home. All the way along the highway, I scolded myself relentlessly. "How could I order those beers and drink them? What a stupid thing to do!" At the time, I did not realize that after God's deliverance, by going back and drinking, I had opened the door for demonic forces to work in my life.

Within a matter of days, I made another compromise. It seemed innocent enough, but I knew better. I wanted to lose weight so I decided to go see a doctor. "Maybe he can give me some diet pills," I said to myself. Here again, I had already promised the Lord way back when I was saved that I would never again take diet pills! I used to take as many as thirty-five a day to get stoned.

"But I'll just take them by a doctor's prescription," I rationalized. "I know the Lord doesn't want me to be fat." So I laid aside my promise to the Lord never to touch another diet pill again. I took them all through January and lost forty pounds. The only other difference I noticed was a little irritability. I was also more energetic and more talkative. But I didn't pay close attention to Kevin as I had before.

Three weeks after he started college in January, we began to see a personality change again. He would do strange things. He would get home, come in and not say much of anything to anyone. He lived in his own little private world. As soon as he'd eaten supper, he would go out of the house. "I'm going to the ridge," he'd say. Or, if he didn't leave the house, he'd go to his room and close himself in for hours with rock and roll music. Calvin and I were pretty sure he'd found some drugs, but we weren't certain.

180

Kevin went to church with us every Sunday and wrote his parole officer faithfully. But trouble was brewing and I knew it. Without really trusting in the Lord, I just didn't know how to stem the tide.

One day in late February, I went to town to do my grocery shopping. On the way home, I drove past the high school and watched Calvin, Jr., play ball. It was such a warm day! Usually at this time of year it would be below freezing, but it was like spring, in the upper sixties. On the spur of the moment, I decided to drive through Kevin's college campus. "Maybe I'll run into him," I thought. And I did. I saw him walking down the sidewalk. I pulled over, smiling and waving, and shouted, "Hello!"

He came over and said, "Hi, Mom. Do you have any money?"

I gave him a careful look. It just so happened I did have $100 I'd withdrawn from the bank earlier that day as a final payment on a surprise bedroom set for Kevin's room. He didn't know about it, and I had planned to pick it up the next day, Saturday, and surprise him with it. Calvin had hired a man to remodel Kevin's upstairs bedroom, and now I wanted to refurnish it.

In my mind, I rationalized that the hundred dollars wasn't really mine. It belonged to the people I was buying the bedroom set from. "No," I answered him, "I don't have any money. I've just returned from the grocery store, and I've spent every dime."

Kevin didn't believe me. His mannerism changed. He became irritable and started yelling at me. He used to be so polite. I observed then that he was high on drugs. I began to cry, and he started walking away.

"Please, Kevin," I called after him, "don't you want

181

to ride home with me?"

And he screamed at me, "No! I'll ride home later with Calvin!"

I drove the car over to Calvin's garage and went to his office and sat down to wait for him. When he entered the door, I said, "Calvin, it's no good. Call Kevin's parole officer. He's back on drugs. I can't stand it; I can't take it. I don't know what I'm going to do." Then I made a statement that I had repeated to many people over the past few months. "I'd rather see him dead than behind bars again, but I just don't know what to do." I couldn't quit sobbing, but I managed to explain to Calvin what had happened.

"Don't worry, Myrle," he encouraged. "I'll talk to Kevin tonight. It'll be all right. You just go on home now and trust the Lord."

I did go home, but I didn't stay there. Instead, I did an odd thing. I made plans to go out for the evening with a lady down the creek. We decided to go to an auction some fifteen miles away in Booneville and then stop off at a little Pentecostal church for a meeting. It was the first time since we moved to Kentucky that I went out without Calvin after dark.

Besides that, I did something else out of the ordinary. As a rule, after making the sixty-mile round trip to Jackson and spending the day grocery shopping, I would have been too worn out to go anywhere. But I knew how to get some extra vitality. Everything was going so badly anyway; "I'll just take an extra diet pill," I said to myself, heading for the medicine cabinet in the bathroom. It picked me up fast, and kept me going until one o'clock the next morning when I fell in bed.

After only a few hours sleep, I got up real early. I

wanted to fix breakfast and then go pick up the furniture I'd bought for Kevin's bedroom. Kevin stepped into the kitchen while I was flipping pancakes. He was himself again. "Mom, I'm sorry. I'm sorry I hurt you. I've been on drugs again for about three weeks. But I can't help it; I just have to have them." He explained how the drugs were available. "There're some boys in the dorm who have it," he said. "Maybe I'll just quit college and stay back here in the hollow where I can't get to them."

"Kevin, I forgive you," I said. "But it's your own two feet that take you over to that dorm where those boys have drugs. Can't you just stay away?"

"I'll try, Mom," he promised. "I'll try."

"Well, we can talk about it later. Because right now," I told him, "I'm going to go pick up some new bedroom furniture for your room. I wanted to surprise you." I was excited about the furniture, and he seemed to be, too. "I'll be back in a couple of hours. In the meantime, Calvin has left a list of chores for you boys to do."

"We'll have them done," Kevin promised, as I walked out the front door.

I'm sure he meant it at the time, but when I came home, I found Calvin, Jr., doing Kevin's chores. He'd already finished his own. "Where's Kevin?" I asked, angrily.

"In his room, Mom," Calvin, Jr., answered.

It was Saturday and Calvin worked until 1:00 P.M. We'd had problems with Kevin before on the weekends, but I usually let Calvin handle it. Today, I had to deal with it, and I tackled it head on.

I stomped down the hall and threw open Kevin's bedroom door. He was sitting on the bed with his back

183

to me. "What's going on?" I said. And he didn't answer.

"Kevin," I ordered, "you go out and help Calvin, Jr., get the furniture out of the truck!"

He still didn't move, so I yelled at him, "Kevin! Get out there and help your brother!"

Then he turned to face me, screaming like an outraged animal. He made a horrible face and began tearing into me verbally, thrashing his arms about furiously. Calvin, Jr., rushed into the room. "Kevin," he said, starting to cry. "You're not going to talk to my mother like this. You're not going to treat her like this after all she's been through." And he made a desperate plea, "Oh, Kevin, why are you blowing it? You're going to go back to prison. Don't you know we love you? Don't you know *I* love you?"

But Kevin just stood there with a stupid grin on his face, staring at us both. "He took some drugs while I was down the creek. He's had them stashed in the house all along," I said to myself with my final hopes for Kevin crashing in around me.

Calvin, Jr., and Kevin carried the furniture in and then Calvin, Jr., got on his motorcycle and went down the road. That left Kevin and me alone. To my dying day, I swear I don't know why it happened or how. But something inside of me snapped. I went to pieces. Within two minutes after Calvin, Jr., rode away, I took our .38 revolver out of Calvin's dresser, walked over to Kevin, and shot him. He died instantly, and it didn't even dawn on me what I'd done. I was not in reality; I was not myself. All I thought about was, "No more worry. No more heartache. He's with the Lord now. We'll have some peace of mind."

Then I jumped in the pickup truck parked out front

184

and went down the road in search of Calvin, Jr. As soon as I saw him, the numbness wore away, and I fell apart. We went to a neighbor's house, and they called the police. Calvin should have been home by then, but he didn't come. Other neighbors went to find him while I laid on a bed in a strange room and cried and cried.

God was nowhere to be found. I tried to pray. But I felt like I was sinking into hell, like my feet were actually in the flames.

Finally, about 5:30 P.M., Calvin was found—he'd been working on some heavy equipment for the magistrate of the county. The police were kind and waited all those hours for him to get there. They told him they had to take me into Jackson and book me for murder. In the Jackson jail, I was fingerprinted, booked and locked up.

It was the darkest day of my life; and I have wished a thousand times I could recall the events of that day. What a wretched night I spent, weeping and praying! I couldn't seem to reach Jesus, or sense the Holy Spirit. I was beside myself. Then, it was as if I began to hear the voices of many, many people outside the walls of my cell, calling my name. I just *knew* who those voices were. What I did shocked a lot of Christians. There were so many I'd gotten to know. I'd given my testimony all over. And as I laid there on that hard cot, crying out to God, He revealed to me that He had raised up an army of His people to bring my name before His throne of grace in intercessory prayer.

The next day I was out on bond and went home. People from Ridgeville—God's people from that precious little church where I'd learned so many biblical truths—drove the 200 miles to be with us in our need. And the Lord was good to me beyond my understanding. There wasn't even a mention of the incident in the local newspaper; only Kevin's death notice.

All I can say is, little by little, I came back into reality. And once again, I began to study the Word of God from Genesis to Revelation. Page by page, He began to deal with me, showing me what a heinous sin I'd committed—a sin against the very image of God. I deserved to die for what I'd done. But as God led me by the hand of the Holy Spirit back through the New Testament, I found the Scriptures of what Christ did for us on the cross. And I knew that though my sin was great, He had died to make me clean and to offer me forgiveness through His shed blood on Calvary.

It was late one night when I got down on my knees in the bedroom and wept aloud, asking God to forgive me for my sin. I opened my Bible in front of me and read aloud David's prayer from Psalm 32:5 (*AMP*): "I acknowledged my sin to You, and my iniquity I did not hide. I said, I will confess my transgressions to the Lord [continually unfolding the past till all is told], then You [instantly] forgave me the guilt and iniquity of my sin."

That night I was able to accept God's forgiveness, but I was not able to forgive myself. The next day, Calvin, who was sharing my trauma, phoned Pastor Shelton in Ridgeville and asked him to meet us at a motel near Ridgeville. "Let's pray for Myrle," he said. "I think she needs some real deliverance and a healing of her mind." Pastor Shelton agreed and Calvin reserved a room at a motel. We drove with Pastor Allen and met Pastor Shelton and an elder from the

Ridgeville church. They ministered to me that afternoon and I never realized all these years how I had let resentment and hatred for myself and others build up inside of me.

Even after I found Christ, I would go to church and never tell any of the brothers and sisters my true feelings. They'd say, "How are you today, Myrle?" and I'd answer, "Just great. Couldn't be better. Hallelujah, praise the Lord!" I'd never share my disappointments or need for prayer over personal slights and hurts. I'd never go to a Christian brother or sister and say, "You hurt my feelings by what you said." And I rarely tried to be reconciled when things went awry.

When Kevin was convicted for breaking and entering into homes, some of my Christian friends were the victims, and they brought him to justice. The whole time he was in the penitentiary my resentments against them grew, but I never told anyone about them. I just let them smolder inside of me.

For many hours in the motel room, as those men of God prayed over me, the Holy Spirit kept bringing to my remembrance all those sins and many others that I had never confessed. Sins that festered. Things that were never brought out in the open before. Hidden things deep down inside of me that I had been carrying around all this time, the pain of past marriages, affairs and rejections, resentments over my days in the detention home and other memories of my childhood that had never been healed. I began confessing to the Lord, starting with resentment against my mother because she gave me up for adoption and ending with a confession of my backsliding during the past three years of trouble with Kevin.

Through those three years, as the resentments and worry built up, I became bitter toward the Lord. I asked Him over and over again, "Why is this happening to me and my son?" I withdrew from Bible reading. My mind pondered heavily on the problems I faced with Kevin.

Prayer became deadwood. I closed up the gifts of the Spirit in my life. And as Kevin got worse, my trust in God's help lessened, so I just stopped having my prayer times. I didn't know how to pray anymore. Finally, because I felt that my Christian friends did not understand what I was going through, my fellowship with them became very superficial. And after Calvin and I moved to Morris Fork, I couldn't bring myself to really pour my heart out to anyone.

Many times I have asked myself, Why did I shoot my boy? I honestly don't know. I had tried to convince myself that I had reacted to the diet pills taken the night before Kevin's death. Some people had suggested that the diet pills may have caused a psychotic aftereffect. Perhaps they were right. I realize now that those pills and the several beers I had with Kevin did a great deal of damage to my spirit and allowed Satan access to my life.

But the problem really didn't start with the diet pills or the beers. My downward trend began when Christian people prosecuted my son and I couldn't forgive them. Resentment against them ate me up. Anger, bitterness, hatred grew in my spirit during those three years of stress and emotional upheaval due to Kevin's drug problem and all I went through because of it. I was pushed to the edge of sanity. To my own undoing, I failed to keep my daily fellowship with the Lord, and all of these things got the upper hand.

If only I had stayed close to Jesus through prayer,

reading His Word and fellowshiping with His children! If only I had trusted Him to take care of Kevin! If only I had not repeated to so many different people, "I would rather see Kevin dead than back in prison." Hindsight tells me now that what we confess with our mouths and believe in our hearts can take root in our lives.

But in spite of the greatness of my despicable sin, the Lord's grace proved greater. There, in the motel room, with a grieving heart, I acknowledged my rebellion and confusion to Him. And as I repented, Jesus' presence— a Presence filled with love and mercy—enveloped me. I could almost feel the touch of His healing balm on every hurt. And I wept and wept as He began to heal the guilt of the past.

I knew that Jesus loved me. And I knew I had received His forgiveness. But even after the pastors, the church elder and Calvin prayed for me, one last wound still remained. The elder sensed it, and said, "Myrle, you have to forgive yourself."

I thought, "That's easy for you to say. Here my baby is gone, and I've done it with my own hand. My precious boy whom I loved so much."

And I wasn't able to forgive myself that night. Not for a long time after that.

Chapter 28

Don't Cry Anymore

My hearing came up about a month later. I was so thankful it didn't drag out.

"Do you want a lawyer?" Calvin asked me.

And I answered, "No."

We had talked it over many times and decided that there is only one thing that's important, and that's the hereafter. We have to tell the truth under all circumstances, no matter what the cost. We had decided to put the whole thing in the Lord's hands. With these thoughts in mind, we went together to answer the indictment.

In the Jackson courthouse, the judge called me into his private chambers to introduce me to the prosecuting attorney. But before we went in Calvin offered again, "I'll get you a lawyer, Myrle. Whatever you want me to do." I looked into his dear face; he'd been such a staunch support, and I loved him so much. "No, Calvin," I said evenly. "Let's just tell it like it is."

"The prosecuting attorney is in there with the judge," Calvin reminded me.

"It doesn't matter. I'll tell the prosecuting attorney

exactly what happened to the best of my ability. He can do what he wants with me."

That's what I did. I told the judge and the prosecuting attorney the whole story, with many tears and much remorse. They were stunned but sympathetic. And they sent me home and told me, "We'll let you know when the trial comes up."

That was on Friday afternoon. The following Monday, Calvin and I went to Jackson to hire a lawyer for the actual trial. The one Calvin knew happened to be at the courthouse, so I waited in the pickup truck while he went inside to find him. While in the courthouse, the prosecuting attorney spotted Calvin and asked, "Is your wife in town today?"

Calvin told him I was. "Go get her and bring her in; court's in session today, so we'll try her right now." At that time, the courts were only in session two weeks out of every two months, so if we didn't have any objections, they wanted to take care of it right away. Even though it was extremely short notice, I wanted everything to be over with as quickly as possible. I wasn't even dressed for court appearance, but because we knew the Lord was in control, I went in anyway, blue jeans and all.

There had been one case in court that morning, so the jury was already in the courthouse. While I waited, each one was asked if they knew me and Calvin or had any personal feelings about the case. Two men were replaced because they were acquaintances of ours.

Finally, the jury filed in and took their seats. The prosecuting attorney stood up and said, "We have investigated this case carefully. We have talked to the arresting officers. We have also talked to the defendant, and we the court feel there is no possible good that can come from putting this woman in the penitentiary.

"She is a good woman, an asset to her community, and we have decided to find her 'not guilty' and we want you, the jury, to find her 'not guilty.'" And he handed them a paper to sign. They signed it, and the verdict handed down was "Not Guilty." The entire procedure took about ten minutes, and I just sat there with red eyes, weeping and marveling at the swiftness by which this miracle was passing before me.

Then the judge spoke. "This woman," he explained, "has suffered enough. We don't want any more said about this matter. In proceedings like this, there are many extenuating circumstances. And this is, in itself, a very unusual case. There is more to it than any of us will ever know. But I don't want it discussed any further, because we the court find this woman, Myrle Morris, not guilty." He brought his gavel down with a loud thud.

I couldn't believe it! He excused Calvin and me from the courtroom, and we went home, dazed by the mercy and loving-kindness of our gracious, heavenly Father.

"Lord," I cried out before Him, "You were with me even though I didn't deserve Your protection. Thank You, Jesus!" To Calvin and me, it meant God had truly forgiven me for what I'd done, because the court could have thrown the book at me. I had gone in and confessed to the state prosecuting attorney! They could have locked me up for a long, long time.

But I received more than I deserved from the Lord. Another chance.

The family had been hurt enough; my children had been crushed, but they forgave me. Although I had forgiveness from God, from society and from my family, there was still a vast chasm between me and the Lord. It was my inability to forgive myself. I despised myself. There were times I contemplated suicide. I didn't know how I could go on living with what I'd done.

Christian people were continuously expressing their love and concern. Pastor McCrane and his wife and the Christian people of Morris Fork came often to pray with me, to minister life to my troubled spirit. In the middle of the night, I would wake up crying as a picture of the whole scene would flash into my mind. Sometimes I would remember the incident in the middle of my work, or while eating at the table. Wherever I was, day or night, when I remembered what I'd done, I would dissolve into tears.

The days unfolded one after another. Spring unfurled into summer, and I kept getting up in the morning and putting one foot in front of the other.

Calvin and I got back into real fellowship. We had a new pastor, Bill Winch, and his wife, Ann. I had the opportunity to share my heart and life with them and we developed a vital relationship very quickly.

Calvin and I also began to read the Bible faithfully, memorizing scriptures, praying frequently and having family devotions together every day. And we began putting the Lord first in *everything*.

And then something happened to take my mind off of my own grief and to try to help someone else. This time it was Calvin's turn to walk through the valley of the shadow.

One Monday in early June, Calvin received word from Phoenix, Arizona, concerning the brutal slaying of his daughter, Mary Sue. A detective called Calvin at his office, having traced him through a newspaper article Mary Sue had among her belongings. The article told how Calvin had been appointed service manager of the car dealership in Jackson.

The news that Mary Sue had been murdered, stabbed in the back with a bread knife, was almost more than Calvin could stand. We had so recently been through tragic occurrences and the aftermath of Kevin's death. And now this. They found the man who had killed her within twelve hours. He had killed himself with a gun and was found in Mary Sue's car. They traced the car back to her apartment, broke in and found her body.

It was a miracle her three little ones weren't with her at the time; she'd sent them to a baby sitter for the day. The baby sitter tried to phone her several times, but got no answer. She assumed Mary Sue was entertaining someone, or had gone out on a date.

Now Calvin walked through the darkest days of his life. But the Lord sent two ministering saints; two brothers in Christ from Ohio. They drove those 200 miles from Ridgeville to Morris Fork just to pray over Calvin and to be with him. By then the word had traveled and people started interceding for Calvin. I can honestly say that I do not know what would have happened to us without the support and love of praying Christian friends who stood beside us through Kevin's and Mary Sue's deaths.

And as the weeks slowly went by, it was through the support of those prayers and the abundant grace and love of God that Calvin and I began to see a ray of hope—the chance for a new beginning.

Chapter 29

A New Beginning

Soon after Mary Sue's death—she was only twenty years old and had never married—Calvin and I became very burdened for the welfare of her children. We wondered where they were and who was taking care of them. The more we talked about them, the greater grew our concern.

I called Mary Sue's mother, who was now living in Michigan, and she told us of the three little boys. The youngest child, Ronnie, six months old, was living with his father in California; the other two boys, Rodney Lamont, two-and-a-half, and Terrence Samuel, four-and-a-half, had been given away to a cab driver in Phoenix.

"I couldn't take care of them," Mary Sue's mother explained. She is disabled and not very well. "I never dreamed you and Calvin would want them," she went on.

"It's something the Lord has put on our hearts," I explained to her. And the more Calvin and I talked about it, the more our love began to build toward the two little orphans. It was a supernatural love that God

197

placed in my heart for these boys I had never seen. Four-and-a-half years previously, when Terrence was born, my attitude was awful. And because the child was half-black, half-white, I'd made the statement, "She's not bringing any illegitimate kids into our home! She's not going to disgrace *this* family!"

How swiftly I had forgotten the circumstances of my own painful past, and how hurt I'd been when my own adoptive mother turned Calvin and me away just before Calvin, Jr., was born.

But now, Calvin and I prayed about the boys and decided we wanted them, that we couldn't live without them, and that this would be what Mary Sue would want. "She would want them raised in a Christian home," I told Calvin. So he paid for the plane ticket for Mary Sue's mother to fly out to Arizona. We sent some money with her to offer the cab driver to let us have the boys. And it was a miracle! He gave them up. For Calvin and me, it was a sign from heaven because we prayed that if God wanted us to have the children, He would open all the doors.

He worked everything out, and made a clear path for their little feet.

The morning of the boys' arrival dawned bright and clear, and I awoke with a new joy to meet it. They were coming *today*, and we were going to meet them! My heart and soul were completely elated with the prospects of welcoming two little toddlers into our family. At 43 years of age I was going to start raising a family all over again! I did have some doubts and fears, but these I pushed forcibly from my mind and went downstairs to fix breakfast.

The sun's rays were just beginning to peek over the

top of the ridge as I stepped into the kitchen and threw back the curtains to allow the full glory of the morning sun to flood the room. Soon it would spread it's golden light to warm the entire valley community of Morris Fork.

"Oh, Jesus," I said softly, "how I love You! And how well I know that if it wasn't for You, I wouldn't be here now enjoying the splendor of this summer day."

How warm the sun felt against my face! For the first time in many agonizing months I looked around our beautiful, isolated log cabin where nature and God's good earth completely surround us. "The babies are going to love it here," I thought to myself. And I began to hum a song of praise as I busily went about the task of preparing breakfast.

Later, at the airport, as the huge plane came down out of the clouds, my heard began to pound. I was both excited and apprehensive. "What am I doing?" I asked myself. "My 'baby,' Calvin, Jr., is fifteen years old. How will I ever raise two lively toddlers? How can I do it?"

"You'll do it with My help," the Lord assured me. *"With My help, Myrle, you can do all things."*

And when the airplane landed, and those tiny fellows came down off the ramp, it was as if they were two angels from heaven. They came, sent by God, and dispersed the gloom around us all. They brought in their childish laughter and sparkle, life, joy and a new beginning.

I started to weep as the Lord began speaking to me clearly, deep inside my being.

"Myrle," He said, *"I'm giving you another chance. I'm giving you an opportunity to be a real mother, to be the mother you've always wanted to be."*

The Lord's gifts are so beyond our imagination. He just knew what I needed to mend my spirit, soul and body. He knew of my sorrow and bitter anguish over Kevin's recent death. He knew my sense of defeat, my sin, my shame. He knew my guilt feelings about Mary Sue, too—how many times I had rejected her before I met the Lord.

I deserved nothing. Yet, in his never ending love and grace, God replaced the two children we'd lost with two precious babies. And in doing so, He began to heal my broken heart.

Chapter 30

A Whisper from Heaven

There was still one loose end to tie up, and how beautifully the Lord arranged it!

It all happened one evening in October while I was sitting in front of the television set, watching the P.T.L. Club with its host, Jim Bakker. His guest that night was Jamie Buckingham, well-known author and speaker. Everything was going along rather smoothly until Jamie Buckingham abruptly stopped speaking and looked directly into the camera.

"There's a woman out there," he said, "whose heart has been so broken. She can't forgive herself for the dastardly thing she's done. I'm here to tell you that *God loves you*, and His Holy Spirit is right there in the room with you now. He wants to minister to you."

Immediately, I knew that his message, directed by the Holy Spirit, was for me. Calvin had just come home from work and quietly entered the bedroom. Calvin, Jr., who had been watching the program with me, left his chair, and they both stood prayerfully beside me. I began to weep.

Jamie Buckingham continued to speak to me.

"Open your heart," he said, "and let the Holy Spirit minister to you in His love. Because there is *nothing* so terrible that God won't forgive."

He began to point out, by the word of knowledge (1 Corinthians 12:8), "There's a big, black cloud that keeps you from receiving what God has for you. And it is unforgiveness. You've accepted God's forgiveness, but you can't forgive yourself." And he began to reason with me, "God has forgiven you, and you're no better than God. So if He has forgiven you, you have to forgive yourself."

Something clicked inside of me, and everything seemed dead center again. "Right on," as the kids say. Oh, the tears that flowed as the sweet Holy Spirit clothed me with His love and righteousness, commanding the darkness to leave by authority of His glorious name! Hallelujah, I was set free!

Since that night, I have been completely liberated of all guilt. It's all on the cross now. God, by His grace and mercy, has completely washed me clean of every putrid stain. I have not had any sleepless nights since that evening. And there have been very few tears shed over the past. God healed me from the inside out.

Yes, I have experienced God's grace, love and mercy. I didn't deserve anything, yet in His grace and forgiveness He presented me with two little children to replace the two we'd lost. And they are so precious, so dear. Every morning I get up and pray, "Thank You, Jesus, for a new day of opportunity . . . opportunity to live and work with You and for You."

One night recently, I held Rodney in my arms and rocked him before tucking him in bed. His face is so shiny and sweet. He reached up his tiny hand and touched my face. "Mommy," he said softly. It was like a whisper from heaven. It brought such joy to me to hear him say that. Truly my cup has been filled to the brim and is spilling over!

I don't want to leave you, my dear reader, without an opportunity to surrender your life to the Lord Jesus Christ. God's Word says, "If we confess our sins, he is faithful and just and will forgive us our sins and purify us from all unrighteousness" (1 John 1:9 *NIV*). Jesus is waiting for you, as He waited and dealt so patiently with me, to open your heart's door and let Him come in. Please, don't make *my* mistake. I had let Him come in and look around, only letting Him sit on the throne of my life now and then. Let Him come in and rule and reign as the King of your life—forever!

Will you pray this simple prayer?

"Dear God, I'm a sinner. Your Word says that if I confess my sins, You are faithful and just to forgive me my sins. Well, I'm confessing. You know all about me. You know when I sit down and when I rise up; every hair on my head is numbered. You know me, and You still love me. That I don't understand, but I believe You came to earth and lived as a man, that You died on the cross for my sins, and that You arose from the dead to assure my victory over sin on this earth.

"Come into my heart, Lord Jesus. I promise to live for You forever! From this day on my choices, my will, my plans are under Your leadership and Your command. I believe, by Your shed blood on Calvary, You have cleansed me of every sin of the past. And I know today—right now—I'm a child of the King. Thank You, Lord! In the name of Jesus, Amen."

Now read the Word, saturate yourself with God's truths. Become a part of a body of believers; fellowship with God's people. Be filled with the Spirit! Tell others what He means to you, and what He's done for you. And may the grace of God keep you and bless your going out and coming in from this day forward. Don't lose sight, ever, of one amazing fact: Jesus loves *you*. Satan may seek to destroy; but Jesus restores!

And in Him we stand *FORGIVEN!*